Romans Understanding God's Grace and Power

Bruce BICKEL
&
Stan JANTZ

HARVEST HOUSE PUBLISHERS

EUGENE, OREGON

Cover by Left Coast Design, Portland, Oregon

Cover photo by Steve Terrill Photography; www.terrillphoto.com

ROMANS: UNDERSTANDING GOD'S GRACE AND POWER
Copyright © 2004 by Bruce Bickel and Stan Jantz
Published by Harvest House Publishers
Eugene, Oregon 97402
www.harvesthousepublishers.com

Library of Congress Cataloging-in-Publication Data

Bickel, Bruce, 1952–
    Romans : understanding God's grace and power / Bruce Bickel and Stan Jantz.
       p. cm. — (Christianity 101)
    ISBN-13: 978-0-7369-0907-5 (pbk.)
    ISBN-10: 0-7369-0907-9 (pbk.)

    1. Bible. N.T. Romans—Commentaries. I. Jantz, Stan, 1952– II. Title. III. Series.
    BS2665.53.B53 2004
    227'.107—dc22

                                    2003022038

Printed in the United States of America

07 08 09 10 11 / DP-CF / 10 9 8 7 6 5 4 3

Contents

A Note from the Authors 5

1. Introduction and Theme 11
   Romans 1:1-17

2. The Reality and Consequence of Sin 23
   Romans 1:18–2:16

3. God's Forgiveness of Sin. 35
   Romans 2:17–3:31

4. Faith for the Ages. 47
   Romans 4

5. Peace with God 59
   Romans 5

6. Freedom in Christ 71
   Romans 6

7. Struggling with Sin. 83
   Romans 7

8. Living in the Spirit. 95
   Romans 8

9. God and Israel 107
   Romans 9–11

10. How to Live as a Christian 121
    Romans 12

11. Living as a Citizen of This World 133
    Romans 13

12. Living in Christian Community. 143
    Romans 14:1–15:13

13. How to Be an Intentional Christian 155
    Romans 15:14–16:27

Dig Deeper. 165

A Note from the Authors

*T*he book of Romans is one of the most profound in all of Scripture. You could spend a lifetime studying it and never finish. At the same time, with a little effort, you will be richly rewarded. No less an authority than Martin Luther said this about Romans:

> *It is worthy not only that every Christian should know it word for word, by heart, but also that he should occupy himself with it every day, as daily bread of the soul.*

We're not suggesting that you *memorize* Romans, but if ever there were a book to *master,* this is the one. "If you really grasp the book of Romans in its totality," writes Ray Stedman, "you will find yourself at home in any other part of the Scriptures." That's why Romans is sometimes called "The Master Key to Scripture."

Just a Little Help

We've taken a different approach from most commentaries and Bible studies in *Romans: Understanding God's*

Grace and Power. Let's face it. Lots of scholarly books will give you the technical theological concepts of the book of Romans. But if you simply want a little something to help you understand Romans and what it means to you personally, then this is the book for you. Each chapter is written to walk you through Romans step-by-step. We don't want to get in the way of your own personal study, but we do want to guide and encourage you.

Christianity 101™ Bible Studies

This Bible study on Romans is part of a series called Christianity 101™ Bible Studies. We've designed this series to combine the biblical content of a commentary with the life applications of a Bible study. By reading this book and answering the questions, you will learn the basics of what you need to know so you will get more meaning from the Bible. Not only that, but you will be able to apply what the Bible says to your everyday Christian life.

And just in case you want even more help in your study of God's Word, we have listed some books that were helpful to us in our study of Romans. You'll find these at the end of the book in a section called "Dig Deeper." In addition, we have put together an online resource exclusively for users of the Christianity 101™ Bible Studies. All you have to do is click on www.christianity101online.com (see page 169 for details).

A Few Suggestions Before You Begin

As you read this book, have your Bible open to Romans so we can do this together. Remember, we aren't your teachers. We are more like trail guides explaining a few things and showing you some points of interest along the way. The Holy Spirit is your teacher, and He's the best. He will show you everything you need to know about Romans and how it applies to your Christian life (1 Corinthians 2:10).

Depending on how you are going to study Romans, here are some things you should keep in mind:

If You Are Studying Romans on Your Own

- Pray and ask God to help you understand His Word.

- Before you begin, read Romans all the way through to get an overview. Don't worry if you don't understand all the concepts right now.

- As you work through each chapter in this Bible study, try to understand the themes of Romans as well as its context in the larger scope of the Bible.

- Write out your answers to the questions and exercises in the "Study the Word" section at the end of each chapter (this will help reinforce what you are learning).

- Thank God for the wonderful riches of His Word, His provision for your life now, and His plans for your future.

If You Are Studying Romans in a Group

- Come prepared to the Bible study by doing everything suggested for individual study.

- Be a willing participant in the discussion, but don't dominate the conversation.

- Encourage and affirm the other people in your group as they talk. Sometimes the best way to do this is to make eye contact and nod your head in an approving manner. (Note: nodding your head as you fall asleep does not qualify as "approving.")

- Be open and honest in your answers. If you don't understand something, admit it! Someone else may have the answer you're looking for.

- Sharing what a particular passage means to you is okay, but first you should try to discover what it means to everyone. Remember, biblical truths aren't different for different people.

- If someone shares something confidential, keep it in the group. At the same time, avoid turning your group Bible study into a gossip session.

- Pray for the other members of your group on a regular basis. Here's how Paul prayed for a group of Christians in his day:

  So we have continued praying for you ever since we first heard about you. We ask God to give you a complete understanding of what he wants to do in your lives, and we ask him to make you wise with spiritual wisdom. Then the way you live will always honor and please the Lord, and you will continually do good, kind things for others. All the while, you will learn to know God better and better (Colossians 1:9-10).

That's our prayer for you as well. So let's get started.

The Christian's Field Manual

Just about every organization—whether it's a company, school, team, charity, or government agency—has a written field manual or a handbook. On one end of the spectrum is the US Army Survival Manual. It's hundreds of pages long because it includes such detailed instructions as "How to Survive in the Arctic by Eating a Seal" (we're not making this up). On the other end is the employee handbook for a well-known department store. It's just one page long and concludes with the sentence: "Use your best judgment at all times." Regardless of the length, field manuals and handbooks are written for one basic purpose: to ensure *survival* and *success*.

Did you know that Christians have a field manual? Well they do, and it just happens to be Romans, the book you're about to study. Romans is one of the most often read books in the Bible because it doesn't just tell us what the Christian life is all about (which is pretty valuable)—it also tells us how to live (which is *really* valuable). Or, to put it another way, Romans tells us what to *believe* as well as how to *behave*. You can't get much more useful and practical than that.

Do you want to *survive* as a Christian in a world that will do everything possible to make you crash and burn? Do you want to *succeed* in your Christian life rather than fail? Then don't just read the book of Romans. Study it for all it's worth!

Chapter 1

Introduction and Theme

Romans 1:1-17

---

*W*hat's *A*head

- ☐ Who Wrote Romans?

- ☐ Why Was Romans Written?

- ☐ What's It All About?

---

*S*ome scholars consider Romans to be the most clear, concise, and comprehensive statement of true Christianity ever written. Romans is valuable because it tells us what our faith is all about. It shows us the most basic problem of the human race: our *sin*. It gives us God's ultimate solution to our sin problem: our *Savior*, Jesus Christ. And it instructs us how to respond to God's wonderful love, grace, and transforming power: our *service*. As you study this remarkable book, you will get to the bedrock of your Christian faith.

Who Wrote Romans?

The book of Romans is actually a letter (also called an *epistle*) written to the church in Rome by Paul the apostle

(1:1). Paul was the greatest missionary the world has ever seen. Paul not only personally carried the Gospel—or *Good News*—of Jesus Christ to the far reaches of the Roman Empire in the first century, but he also established the foundation of the Christian belief system through his letters to churches and to a few individuals. Romans is one of nine letters Paul wrote to the young churches in Asia Minor (present-day Turkey), Greece, and Italy. Paul also wrote four letters to three different people.

The Letters of Paul

To Churches	Location	Present Day	Date
Romans	Rome	Italy	A.D. 57
1 and 2 Corinthians	Corinth	Greece	55–57
Galatians	Galatia	Turkey	49
Ephesians	Ephesus/ Asia Minor	Turkey	60 or 61
Philippians	Philippi	Greece	61
Colossians	Colossae	Turkey	60
1 and 2 Thessalonians	Thessalonica	Greece	51–52

To Individuals	Relationship to Paul	Date
1 and 2 Timothy	Disciple and close friend	64–67
Titus	Paul's representative to Crete	64
Philemon	Member of the church at Colossae	60

These first-century churches and people have long since faded from the landscape, but the letters live today as brilliant and practical guides to living the Christian life. How did one man—who was short and bald with a crooked nose and some kind of physical affliction—have such a profound influence on the Christian faith? He was a part of God's wonderful plan.

Before He Was Paul

Paul (his Roman name) was born Saul (his Jewish name) in Tarsus, an important commercial city that was the capital of a Roman province. Saul was a Roman citizen by birth, but culturally and religiously he was thoroughly Jewish. Between the ages of 13 and 20, Saul moved from Tarsus to Jerusalem, where he trained to be a rabbi under the famed master-teacher Gamaliel, whose grandfather founded the Pharisaic school. "At his feet," Paul once told a crowd of Jews, "I learned to follow our Jewish laws and customs very carefully. I became very zealous to honor God in everything I did, just as all of you are today" (Acts 22:3).

Saul was zealous, all right. So zealous that he became one of the fiercest persecutors of the early church. Saul stood by as Stephen was stoned to death (Acts 8:1). He became a man whose goal was to "destroy the Lord's followers" (Acts 9:1). Then something dramatic happened to change Saul's life and the life of the church. Jesus met him on the road to Damascus through a blinding light and a voice that called out, "Saul! Saul! Why are you persecuting me?" (Acts 9:4).

Saul was spiritually transformed, and he eventually came to be known as Paul. More importantly, he became the Lord's "chosen instrument" to take the Good News of Jesus "to the Gentiles and to kings, as well as to the people of Israel" (Acts 9:15). This is exactly what Paul had in mind as he wrote his letter to the Roman church (1:1).

Why Was Romans Written?

Even though Paul was a Roman citizen, he had never been to Rome. He had never met most of the believers in Rome, and he had nothing to do with founding the church there. He knew that the believers in Rome— mostly Gentiles with some Jews sprinkled in—were growing in their faith (1:8), but he also knew they needed his encouragement and some solid teaching (1:11). Paul had been praying constantly for the Roman Christians, and now he was anxious to travel to Rome to visit them. In one sense, Paul wrote this letter to prepare the way for his visit.

So why did Paul write such a detailed letter to the Romans if he was planning to be in Rome soon? Probably because he knew his life was in danger. After spending three relatively peaceful years in Ephesus (A.D. 53–56), Paul traveled to Corinth in Greece, where he stayed for three months. While he was there he discovered a plot to kill him (Acts 20:3). Then, as if to add confirmation to what Paul was hearing, the Holy Spirit repeatedly told him that his future would include "jail and suffering" (Acts 20:23).

Paul was not afraid of such grim prospects—he said his life was worthless unless he was using it to tell others "the Good News about God's wonderful kindness and love" (Acts 20:24)—but he was also practical. He knew he might not make it to Rome. So while he was in Corinth, Paul wrote a detailed letter to the Roman church that contained a systematic and comprehensive treatment of what this Good News of Jesus Christ is all about. He wanted not only to encourage the Roman Christians but also to teach them.

$\mathcal{R}$omans at a $\mathcal{G}$lance

Author:	Paul the Apostle
Date written:	A.D. 57
Written to:	The church at Rome and all believers everywhere
Type of book:	An epistle, or letter
Setting:	Paul wrote this letter while in Corinth before he traveled to Jerusalem, where he was arrested and imprisoned.
Purpose:	Paul wanted to prepare the Roman believers for his visit to Rome and to strengthen them in their faith.
Major themes:	The *sin* of humankind, the *salvation* of Christ, the *sanctification* of believers, the *sovereignty* of God, and the *service* of the church.

Challenges in Rome

In the first century, Rome was the largest and most influential city in the world. As the center of a vast empire that reached from Arabia to Britain, Rome was home to more than a million people. Rome was a great secular city, and it was also a very religious city—although few people there worshiped the living God of Scripture. The Romans were polytheistic. They worshiped many gods, including the gods of mythology. Many Roman citizens also worshiped their emperor, a practice known as *Caesar worship.*

The Christians as well as the Jews were at a great disadvantage in Roman society. Because they refused to worship the Romans' gods in favor of the one true God, they were considered atheists. Furthermore, the Christians pledged their allegiance first to God, not the Roman state. Clearly the Christians stood out, which didn't help their cause any when Nero, the emperor who ruled at the time Paul wrote Romans, unleashed an extensive and brutal program of persecution against Christians from A.D. 64 until his death in A.D. 68. Historians believe that Paul was beheaded under Nero's reign of terror.

What's It All About?

Paul was convinced that the Roman church could become a world missionary center, sending out committed believers who would continue his work of taking the Good News of Jesus to the farthest corners of the Roman Empire. Because of what Jesus had done for him, Paul felt obligated to tell people in all cultures about what Jesus could do for them (1:14). And he wanted the Roman believers to share this same sense of obligation and urgency. That's why this magnificent letter is so systematic and comprehensive. Paul's desire was for the Christians in Rome and believers everywhere to live the Christian life and share it with others.

The Themes of Romans

The major themes of Romans are foundational to your Christian life. Master these concepts, and you will be in proper relationship with God, knowing the way He wants you to live. Overlook these basic truths, and you will be frustrated in your Christian life.

> *Sin*—Sin is not doing what God wants us to do. It's falling short of His perfect standard (3:23). Nobody is without sin, and since sin leads to death (6:23), the human race is in a desperate place.
>
> *Salvation*—We can't satisfy God's perfect standard, but Jesus can. God loved us so much that He sent Jesus to accept the death penalty of sin in our place. And He did this while we were sinners (5:8). By accepting God's free gift of salvation through faith, we can have eternal life (6:23).
>
> *Sanctification*—This is a lofty theological word (LTW), but the concept is pretty easy to understand. God, who is wholly holy, can relate to us only if we are holy. And the only way we can be holy is to belong to Jesus Christ (1:6) because only Jesus can set us apart from sin. He literally makes us holy by delivering us from a life dominated by sin (7:24-25).
>
> *Sovereignty*—Here's another LTW. Even though every person has sinned (3:23), and even though the world groans under sin's weight (8:22), God is still completely in control and completely in charge. He is still sovereign. God loves and cares about all people, and He is totally fair in all He

does. God's sovereignty guarantees that nothing can ever separate us from Christ's love (8:35-37).

Service—God doesn't save us just so we can sit and do nothing. By saving us, He calls us into a life of service to Him and others. Your goal should be to "let God transform you into a new person by changing the way you think. Then you will know what God wants you to do, and you will know how good and pleasing and perfect his will really is" (12:2).

The Good News About Christ

In the first nine verses, Paul uses the phrase *Good News* four times (1:1-3,9). Just what is the Good News? Paul explains in Romans 1:16-17, two verses that express the theme of Romans and form the heart of Christianity. Paul is not ashamed of this Good News about Christ for two reasons:

- *The Good News is the power of God to transform lives (1:16).* Christianity isn't some man-made religion or philosophy with no power. It contains the power of God, and He is able to save everyone who believes.

- *We receive the Good News by faith (1:17).* The only way to be made right with God is to receive God's salvation gift by faith. And what is faith? As Dr. James Boice explains, "Faith is not a work. It is believing God. It is opening a hand to receive the righteousness of Christ that God offers."

▨ ▨ ▨

Study the Word

1. Have you ever read a field manual or an organiza-
    tion's employee handbook? Did it help you better
    understand the organization and what was expected
    of you? If so, how? If not, why not?

2. As a Roman citizen, did Paul have any privileges or
    advantages? Do you think his citizenship was ever a
    hindrance? If you can, find in the Bible where Paul's
    citizenship probably saved his life. (Hint: Look in the
    book of Acts.)

3. Give a one-paragraph summary of what the Good
    News is all about.

4. How did Paul's training in the Pharisaic school help him relate to Jews? How did it help him relate to Gentiles? With his thorough training in all things Jewish, why do you think Jesus directed Paul to take the Good News message to the Gentiles?

5. Christians were called atheists in the Roman culture. Today Christians are likely to be labeled intolerant. Is that a fair description? Why or why not?

Should Christians ever be intolerant? How about tolerant?

How would you respond to someone who accused you of being intolerant because you are a Christian?

6. Romans 1:16-17 has sometimes been called the best summary of the Good News in the entire Bible. If you can, read these verses in at least three different Bible translations. If you are a Christian, list three insights that will help you better explain your faith to an unbeliever. If you aren't yet a Christian, do you find anything about those two verses compelling? Is anything about them confusing?

7. Read Habakkuk 2:4, the verse that Paul quotes in Romans 1:17. Why does the prophet say that people who trust in themselves are "crooked" (NLT) or "puffed up" (NIV)? Why are people who live by faith considered righteous?

Spiritual Sickness

Consider the following scenario. Suppose you have a life-threatening illness, but you refuse to admit you are sick. Instead of seeing a doctor who has a surefire cure for your condition, you choose to deny your problem and ignore the solution. As far as you are concerned, you are completely healthy. In reality, you would be...

a) wise to ignore reality
b) blissfully ignorant
c) a very foolish person

Okay, so this is a no-brainer...or is it? Certainly in the natural world nobody would willingly choose death over life, but what about the spiritual realm? That's an entirely different story. The world is full of people who insist they are perfectly healthy when in fact they have a fatal spiritual disease. In this section of Romans, Paul writes directly to this audience, and he doesn't pull any punches.

Chapter 2

The Reality and Consequence of Sin

Romans 1:18–2:16

---

*W*hat's *A*head

- ☐ The Wrath of God (1:18-23)

- ☐ The Revelation of God's Wrath (1:24-32)

- ☐ God's Judgment of Sin (2:1-16)

*I*n the first part of Romans 1, Paul asserts that God is powerful enough (1:16) and righteous enough (1:17) to save anyone who believes. Because of what God has done for him, Paul feels obligated to tell all people, whether educated or uneducated, about the Good News of Jesus.

If only everyone were wise enough to realize his or her need to be saved from sin's death penalty. Witnessing to people would be so much easier! But that's not the way it is. The world is filled with people who deny their fatal sin sickness and ignore God's life-giving solution. And what is God's response to people who willfully refuse the solution He has so graciously offered and choose instead to live in their sin? That's what Paul is going to tell us.

In this section, Paul explains God's response to sin in three straightforward steps: First, he talks about the wrath of God against sin. Then he shows how God reveals His wrath. Finally, Paul gives us the nature of God's judgment of sin.

The Wrath of God (1:18-23)

Paul wrote his letters to the believers so they could be read aloud in church. We still carry on this tradition today whenever someone reads aloud from the Bible. With that in mind, imagine yourself sitting on a wooden bench in a room somewhere in first-century Rome as your pastor reads a letter from Paul, the great missionary. The first part of the letter is music to your ears as Paul describes the faith of your church in flattering terms. "He knows about our faith," you whisper to a friend sitting next to you. "Well, you know what they say," your friend responds. "The righteous shall live by faith." You think for a minute, and then whisper back, "Yes, we certainly are righteous," and then you both nod approvingly.

Suddenly the tone of Paul's letter changes. Your pastor begins reading phrases like "wrath of God" and "wickedness" and "their foolish hearts were darkened." Oh my. What's this all about? Who could Paul possibly be talking about? Surely not us. We're righteous! You start to think about all those pagans crowded into the Coliseum watching today's featured gladiator match between the Titans and the Raiders. It's bad enough that they sell fermented grapes over there, but do they have to have those games on a Sunday? How wicked! After daydreaming for a bit, you focus again on Paul's letter. This "wrath of God" business has you very curious.

The Nature of God's Wrath (1:18)

The idea that God is wrathful bothers a lot of people today, including many Christians. How can a God of love get angry? How can a loving God judge and punish people? Good questions! You need to know the answers.

Yes, God is love (1 John 4:8). But He is also holy (1 Peter 1:16), and He is a God of justice (Deuteronomy 32:4). Don't make the mistake of favoring one attribute of God over another. His personality is in perfect balance. So, while we praise the God of love and mercy, we also acknowledge and respect—dare we say, *fear*—a holy God who cannot and will not tolerate sin and evil.

If it's any comfort (and it should be), you will notice in the text that the wrath (or anger) of God is not directed toward people but against the "godlessness and wickedness" that people do. God hates what is wrong (Psalm 45:7). It makes him angry. But His anger isn't like human anger, which is personal, emotional, and often malicious. God's anger is completely objective, appropriate, and just. As John R.W. Stott writes, God's wrath "is his holy hostility to evil."

The Object of God's Wrath (1:18-23)

If God's wrath is directed to sin and evil, where does that leave those of us who have accepted His solution for sin, Jesus Christ? Since we are still capable of sin, is God still angry at the sin that's in all of us? In principle, yes. God opposes the evil that's in us, but in practice He is revealing His wrath against specific people: those who "push the truth away from themselves." These aren't people who merely sin. These are people who know better, and yet they sin anyway. As we're going to see later in this chapter, God also directs His wrath against those who claim to know Him personally and yet continue to willingly sin (so don't get too smug yet), but for now we're going to concentrate on people who deliberately ignore the truth about God.

Verses 19 and 20 are absolutely key to understanding how God has made Himself known to every single person who has ever lived. "The truth about God" has four characteristics. It is...

- *Instinctive*—No one has to tell us that God is real because God has put this truth in every person.

- *Visible*—Everyone can observe the wonder and grandeur of the universe.

- *Reasonable*—When you carefully observe the world, you are reasonable to conclude that a supernatural, super-intelligent, powerful being created it.

- *Descriptive*—The order and beauty of the universe point to a loving, caring God rather than to an undirected, mechanistic, random series of unrelated events.

God has wonderfully and completely revealed Himself to humankind through His created universe. God has also planted the truth about Himself into the heart of every person. Because of what God has done, no one will ever be able to say, "But I never knew God was real!" We will have no excuses on Judgment Day.

Can Knowledge Lead to Salvation?

This knowledge about God as revealed in the universe is sometimes called *general revelation* because it is common to all people in general. This knowledge can lead us to a recognition that God is real, and it can even tell us that we need a Savior, but this knowledge alone can't save us. As Paul stated in 1:17, we are saved only through faith in Jesus Christ. Still, the knowledge God has given us is enough to get us started on our spiritual journey, and it is enough to condemn us.

Instead of acknowledging the existence of God and thanking Him for this wonderful world He created for our benefit (1:21), people have chosen instead to glorify idols and images (1:23). In some cultures and in some religions, these are literally carved idols. But Paul's description could also apply to any material things that become the objects of our worship, such as cars, companies, and careers. Even things that are worthwhile, such as family, recreation, and education, can become objects of God's wrath if they replace Him as the most important thing in our lives.

The Revelation of God's Wrath (1:24-32)

Paul tells us how God's wrath is revealed in three different sections, each beginning with the phrase "gave them over" (1:24,26,28 NIV). The utter horror of God's wrath isn't that it's expressed in lightning bolts, earthquakes, fatal diseases, or terrorist attacks (although that's what most people think). No, it's something much worse than that. God doesn't express His wrath by causing things to happen. Rather, He simply allows sinful humanity to do what comes naturally, and that's to sin. In these verses Paul paints a picture of self-centered, godless people living their lives for themselves with no regard for their Creator. As you will see, it's not a pretty picture.

Sinful Desires (1:24-25)

When people disregard God and refuse to let Him run their lives, their natural sinful desires take over. The most open and obvious expression of these desires is in the area of sexual behavior, but sinful desires can also include anything people lust after, whether it's people or things. People let their desires run wild because they exchange "the truth of God for a lie" (1:25 NIV), leading them to serve and worship the creation rather than the Creator.

The World's Biggest Lie

Do you want to know the biggest lie in the world? Number one on the all-time lie list was first told by Satan in the Garden of Eden, who convinced Eve she wouldn't die if she disobeyed God. Not only will you not die, Satan told her, but you'll be rewarded. "You will become just like God, knowing everything, both good and evil" (Genesis 3:4-5). Eve fell for it, and ever since, people have been buying into the Big Lie. Rather than responding to the truth about God, they try to be like God themselves.

Shameful Lusts (1:26-27)

Here Paul gets more specific. God gives people over not only to their sinful desires but to their shameful acts as well. The position Paul takes in these two verses isn't popular in today's culture. Some in the church argue that Paul's warning to the Romans can't be applied to our enlightened and tolerant culture today. Don't be fooled. If anything, the practices of the people in the Roman culture—characterized by excessive violence, preoccupation with wealth, and immorality—are like a mirror for our own culture. God was angry at these sins then, and He's angry at them now.

A Depraved Mind (1:28-32)

These last few verses of Romans 1 should chill us to the bone. When people don't consider God to be worthwhile, when people remove God from the public square and their own private thinking, this is the result: depraved behavior coming out of depraved minds. This is the result of humankind declaring its independence from God. The problem is that this isn't freedom at all. People think they are fully enlightened and free because they are able to do what they please. In fact, they are slaves to their own dark hearts.

God's Judgment of Sin (2:1-16)

So there you are in first-century Rome, listening to Paul's letter. Your eyes are wide open and your jaw has dropped to the floor as you listen to the description of immoral excess. You are glad the letter isn't talking about you and your righteous friend. Then the tone shifts and your own seat starts to get a little hot as Paul turns the spotlight of God's anger from the sins of depraved people who have shut God out of their lives to the sins of people who claim to love God.

The message in this section is that all people are sinners, and therefore none of us have any excuses. None of us are good enough, no matter how self-righteous we feel, to escape God's judgment on our own. Without faith in Jesus and total dependence on His salvation, we are just as doomed as those flagrant sinners out there.

And that's another thing: We need to stop judging others for their sins when we are harboring sins of our own. We aren't in a contest to determine whose sins are less offensive to God. All sins offend God and invite His judgment, which Paul characterizes in five ways:

God's Judgment Is Truthful *(2:1-2)*

Human judgment is biased and prejudiced. God's judgment is based on facts, and He knows every fact about every person.

God's Judgment Is Universal *(2:3-4)*

No one is worthy of escaping God's judgment, and no court is higher than God's. God's laws have no loop-holes.

God's Judgment Is Inevitable *(2:5-6)*

Sometimes people respond to the notion of God's judgment with defiance. They stubbornly shake their fist at God, believing somehow that they are tough enough and self-willed enough to beat God at His own game. This can even happen in the lives of Christians, but it's a futile and self-destructive attitude. Every person will face God's judgment (Hebrews 9:27).

God's Judgment Is Impartial *(2:7-11)*

If it's any consolation, no one gets a free pass or any favors from God. He shows favoritism to no one. However, God does show *favor*. Those who persist in doing good will receive eternal life. Does this mean that good works can save us? Not in the least. Paul makes clear that only by God's grace are we saved, not by our good works (Ephesians 2:8-9). However, when God saves us, He saves us so we can do good things (Ephesians 2:10). The good Paul is talking about here in Romans is the result of our life in Christ, and the persistence is the steady, forward progression to spiritual maturity that should characterize the life of every believer. As James wrote, "Faith that doesn't show itself by good deeds is no faith at all—it is dead and useless" (James 2:17).

God's Judgment Is Thorough (2:12-16)

Here Paul makes a distinction between those "who sin apart from the law" (this refers to *Gentiles,* or non-Jews) and those "who sin under the law" (these are Jews). Gentiles will be judged, not by their failure to keep the law, but by their failure to acknowledge the God who has revealed Himself in the world (1:20). Jews will be judged by the law because they know what the law says. The bottom line is that God will judge all people—Gentiles and Jews, men and women, religious and non-religious—through Jesus Christ.

That's the bad news. The Good News is that God has offered a way to be saved from His judgment through Jesus Christ, and this also applies to all people—Gentiles and Jews, men and women, religious and non-religious. God shows no favoritism to those He judges, and He also shows no favoritism to those He saves.

■ ■ ■

Study the Word

1. How often is Scripture read out loud in your church? Give three practical benefits to hearing the Word of God read out loud on a regular basis.

2. Why does the idea of a wrathful God bother unbelievers? Why does it bother believers? Why must God be wrathful against sin?

3. Give an example of how "the truth about God" is...

   • instructive

   • visible

   • reasonable

   • descriptive

4. Explain this statement: The knowledge about God as revealed in the universe is not enough to save us, but it is enough to condemn us.

5. How do people buy into the Big Lie these days? Who or what tells this lie most often? Why does this lie lead to sinful desires? Give an example.

6. Who is Paul describing when he talks about people who "persist in doing what is good" (2:7)? Who are those who "keep on sinning" (2:9)? Can a believer keep on sinning? For how long?

7. Explain the difference between God's showing *favoritism* (which He does not do) and *favor* (which He does).

8. Can people have faith that is "dead and useless"? What kind of faith would that be?

No Excuses

Whenever people are confronted with their own sin and shame, they have a tendency to make excuses. This is nothing new. When God confronted Adam with his sin, Adam pointed at Eve and said, "It was the woman you gave me who brought me the fruit, and I ate it." When God asked Eve why she did it, she said, "The serpent tricked me." (Literal translation: "The devil made me do it.") People faced with their own sin will do anything to deflect the blame. And they will go to great lengths to make themselves look good—as if they could somehow fool God.

Paul continues with his message that every person is responsible and will one day be held accountable for his or her sin. And no amount of finger pointing or shadow boxing is going to help. The only thing we humans have going for us is God's forgiveness. But that counts for a whole lot.

Chapter 3

God's Forgiveness of Sin

Romans 2:17–3:31

 What's Ahead

- ☐ Misplaced Trust (2:17-29)

- ☐ God Is Faithful (3:1-8)

- ☐ We Are All Sinners (3:9-20)

- ☐ We Are Forgiven (3:21-31)

*S*o far in his letter to the Romans, Paul has been writing to the whole congregation (Gentiles and Jews alike), but now he directs his attention to the Jews. That doesn't mean all the Gentiles can take a break and tune out. What Paul tells us about God and His relationship to His chosen people applies to everyone.

Misplaced Trust (2:17-29)

The nation of Israel—known collectively as the Jews—holds a very special place in God's heart. The Jews are God's chosen people. As a part of God's magnificent plan to restore sinful people to a right relationship with

Him, God made an agreement (biblical word: *covenant*) with Abraham that included these promises (see Genesis 12:1-3):

- His descendants—the Jews—would become a great nation.

- The land of Canaan would be their homeland.

- All humankind would be blessed by one of his descendents.

By every measurement, the Jews were (and still are) a great people. This special relationship with God and the multipronged promise of blessing set them apart. The only problem was that many Jews believed these blessings were like privileges that put them a few notches above everyone else (namely, the Gentiles). Even more, they believed that God was cutting them more slack than anyone else when it came to obeying and serving Him. Rather than putting their trust in God, they trusted their heritage, their knowledge, and their ritual practices to save them. Paul shows the Jews—and us too—the futility of putting your trust in anything except God.

*W*ho *W*ere the *J*ews?

The term *Jew* comes from *Judah,* a tribe of Israel that was promised a unique place of leadership (Genesis 49:8-10). The root meaning of *Judah* is *praise*. The Jews enjoyed a special assignment from God to bring Him glory among the nations (Isaiah 49:1-3).

Trusting Your Heritage (2:17)

Despite a history that included slavery and oppression, the Jews were intensely proud of their heritage. Rather than praising God for His goodness and grace, they felt special and superior. Rather than thanking God for His blessings and favor, they saw themselves as righteous.

How about you? Do you have a Christian heritage? Do you take it for granted, or do you thank God for His goodness and grace? Some people believe that just because they grew up in the church or were baptized as a child, they have a one-way ticket to heaven. Are you relying on your spiritual heritage for your salvation, or have you made a deliberate choice to accept God's plan to save you though Jesus? We must never fall into the trap of believing that our heritage or position allows us to escape God's judgment.

> Does being born into a Christian family make one a Christian? No! God has no grandchildren.
>
> —*Corrie ten Boom*

Trusting Your Knowledge (2:18-24)

Nobody knew God's law better than the Jews, which in itself was a wonderful thing. The problem was that they had come to trust in their knowledge of the law even more than they trusted God. They placed high value on learning and teaching the law. They saw themselves as a guiding light to the lowly Gentiles, who they referred to condescendingly as "blind" and "lost in darkness."

Besides their smug attitude, the Jews didn't do what they taught others to do. They didn't practice what they preached (these were the same kind of people Jesus called "hypocrites"). Even worse than failing to do what was right, these proud Jews actually broke the law, bringing dishonor to God.

*W*hat *W*as the *L*aw?

The term *law* or *God's law* referred to the five books of Moses (called the Pentateuch); the books of history, poetry and wisdom (called the writings); and the prophets. John MacArthur writes: "The law encompassed all of God's revelation until that time."

Here again, we have to take a look at ourselves. Today we have all of God's Word, not just the Old Testament. Furthermore, we have the Holy Spirit, sent by Jesus to guide us into all truth (John 16:13). What happens when we claim to be Christians and we say that we read and follow God's Word, and yet we flagrantly disobey what it says? How does that make us look? Worse, how does it make God look? Paul used a pretty strong word to describe the result. He said the world "blasphemes" the name of God because of us (2:24). *Ouch!*

*T*he *G*reatest *C*ommandment

A religious leader once asked Jesus to name the most important commandment in the law. Jesus told him, "You must love the Lord your God with all your heart, all your soul, and all your mind." And there's more. "Love your neighbor as yourself" (Matthew 22:37-39). So what happens when we don't obey God by loving Him and each other? Jesus said that the world has every reason to doubt we are His genuine followers (John 13:34-35).

Trusting Your Rituals (2:25-29)

Paul now shines the glare of his arguments on the sacred Jewish ceremony of circumcision. John MacArthur explains that God had instituted circumcision as "a mark of His covenant with Abraham and his descendants." Circumcision was essentially an act of obedience to God and a reminder to Jews of their special relationship to Him.

The problem was that the Jews had come to see circumcision as a badge of honor. They thought the outward symbol was enough to please God even when they were disobeying God in other ways. Paul jumps on this and says in no uncertain terms that a physical ritual doesn't make them true Jews. "No, a true Jew is one whose heart is right with God. And true circumcision is not a cutting of the body but a change of heart produced by God's Spirit" (2:29).

What a powerful principle! All of our human efforts, rituals, and practices aren't what make us right with God. It's the inner attitude of our heart. We need to have the attitude of David, who cried out to God:

> *You would not be pleased with sacrifices, or I would bring them. If I brought you a burnt offering, you would not accept it. The sacrifice you want is a broken spirit. A broken and repentant heart, O God, you will not despise* (Psalm 51:16-17).

God Is Faithful (3:1-8)

Paul makes two very interesting points to open Romans 3. First, he reminds his fellow Jews that being one of God's chosen people has tremendous advantages:

"The Jews were entrusted with the whole revelation of God" (3:2). Their job was to preserve and protect the Scriptures until the coming of Jesus, who fulfilled everything the prophets predicted (Hebrews 1:1-2). Second, Paul reminds his readers that even though some of them were unfaithful, God has always been faithful (3:3). Even though they broke their promises to God, He did not break His promises to them.

Paul then broadens his focus to include three very important concepts that include the whole world.

1. Although everyone in the world has sinned, God is true (3:4).

This is a very important concept to grasp, because someday you're going to run into someone—if you haven't already—who believes that a loving and powerful God and an evil world can't coexist. They will argue that a loving God wouldn't allow evil, and an all-powerful God would stop it. The truth is that God is a loving God, and because He loves us He allows us to make our own choices even though we can choose to disobey Him. God is also a powerful God who will someday deal with evil completely. This is when God "will judge all people according to what they have done" (2:6).

2. God is qualified to judge the world (3:5-6).

People often question God's ability to judge the world fairly. They get into a circular argument, as Paul points out, that goes something like this: If sin brings out the best in God—and it did because it caused Him to send Jesus to earth to save us—then how can He judge sinners, who are responsible for the sin that brings out the best in Him? You can't win an argument like that because it's an illogical question. (Here's another illogical question: Can God make a rock so heavy He can't lift it?) You can't answer such a question because it doesn't deal with reality. With God, the reality is that He is completely just and fair. Yes, our sin brings out God's righteousness, but it doesn't detract from His ability to judge fairly.

3. We shouldn't continue to sin just to make God look good (3:7-8).

This ludicrous conclusion follows the illogical question posed above. Yet this is the way some people view sin. They figure, God is going to forgive me, so I'll just do this thing one more time, and then one more time after that. That's a difficult and troubling way to live. Paul will deal with it more in Romans 7.

We Are All Sinners (3:9-20)

Paul uses Scripture to back up his claim in 3:9 that "all people, whether Jews or Gentiles, are under the power of sin." Quoting from the Psalms and Isaiah, he brilliantly affirms that sin is universal. This is a picture of what theologians call *total depravity*, which has two aspects:

- The entire human race is sinful (3:10-12).
- Each person is completely sinful (3:13-18).

This doesn't mean we are as bad as we can be. It means, as R.C. Sproul writes, "there is no part of us that is left untouched by sin." Our throat, tongue, lips, mouth, feet, and eyes are all infected by the sin virus.

The human race has no answer for this indictment. We're all out of excuses. We are left with no way to work our way to heaven. Paul deals with this option in verses

19 and 20. No one can ever be made right by doing what the law commands because none of us can keep it.

We Are Forgiven (3:21-31)

Okay, enough bad news. Now for the Good News. God has shown us a different way to be right in His sight. We aren't saved by obeying the law but by accepting God's amazing grace. Romans 3:22 is the heart of the Good News message:

> *We are made right in God's sight when we trust in Jesus Christ to take away our sins. And we all can be saved in this same way, no matter who we are or what we have done.*

All the elements of what being saved means are in this verse:

- Jesus is the only way to get right with God.
- Salvation is available to every person equally.
- You can be saved regardless of what you have done.

And just to make sure we get the point, Paul reminds us again that everyone has sinned. Every single person is in need of being saved because no one can meet God's perfect standard (3:23).

Right in His Sight (3:24-26)

The idea that we can be declared "not guilty" is a theological concept called *justification*. Everett Harrison writes in his commentary on Romans: "To be justified includes the truth that God sees the sinner in terms of his relation to his Son, with whom he is well pleased."

You see, God can find no goodness in us, no reason for declaring us righteous. So He must look to Jesus, who is righteous and worthy.

In the great courtroom of heaven, we stand accused of treason against God, the great Judge. All the witnesses have been called, and the verdict is in: guilty. We deserve the death penalty. "Yet now God in his gracious kindness declares us not guilty. He has done this through Christ Jesus, who has freed us by taking away our sins" (3:24). That's what being justified means.

Only by Faith (3:27-31)

Romans 3:27-28 runs parallel to Ephesians 2:8-9. Our acquittal—our salvation—is not based on our good behavior but on the grace of God through the work of Jesus, which we accept by faith. To be clear, our faith doesn't save us—God is the one who saves—but it is the means by which we accept God's merciful "not guilty" verdict.

Faith is important for at least three reasons:

- Faith takes human effort out of the salvation equation.

- Faith gives glory to God rather than to us.

- Faith is based on our relationship with God, not our efforts for God.

At the same time, faith does not eliminate the law. Our works are not involved in the process of justification and salvation, but works are the result of the faith that appropriates those things. That's what Paul means when he writes, "only when we have faith do we truly fulfill the law" (3:31).

■ ■ ■

Study the Word

1. What are the spiritual advantages of being Jewish? What does Paul mean when he says "the Jews were entrusted with the whole revelation of God"?

2. Talk about (or describe on paper) your spiritual heritage. Has it been an advantage or a disadvantage in your life?

3. What "sacrifices" do we try to make in order to gain God's favor?

4. Have you resolved the reality of a loving God with the reality of evil in the world? How?

5. Explain the difference between these two statements:
   • We sin because we are sinners.
   • We are sinners because we sin.

Which one more accurately describes the human condition?

6. Read Romans 3:10-12. What does the Scripture mean when it says, "No one is seeking God"? Are there exceptions to this? If not, why are some churches "seeker sensitive"? If people aren't seeking God when they go to church, what are they seeking?

7. How does having a greater appreciation for your sin give you a greater appreciation for God's justification?

8. Explain what Paul means when he writes, "Only when we have faith do we truly fulfill the law."

*Y*our *L*ife *L*edger

When we hear the terms *credit* and *debit,* most of us think of those little plastic cards we carry in our wallets. To an accountant, however, the terms take on a different meaning. Someone who works with numbers thinks in terms of a ledger, which is a page with two columns. On the left-hand side of the ledger the debits to the account are recorded. The credits are recorded on the right-hand side.

With that in mind, think of your own life as a ledger (Okay, we know you're much more valuable than a piece of paper, but go with us on this one). On the left side of your life ledger are your debits. Think of these as the sins you have committed. On the right side are your credits. These are the good things you have done. When thinking about God and Judgment Day, many people believe that they will make it to heaven if the credits on their life ledger add up to more than their debits. But that's not what the Bible says.

As Paul has already demonstrated, we all have a sin debit that no amount of human-generated credit can overcome. Our only hope to get into heaven is for God to give us enough credit to erase our insurmountable debt. And that's exactly what God has done. You're going to find out exactly how God has done this—and learn more about justification—as you study Romans 4.

Chapter 4
Faith for the Ages
Romans 4

*W*hat's *A*head

- By Faith, Not Works (4:1-8)

- By Faith, Not Ritual (4:9-12)

- By Faith, Not the Law (4:13-17)

- The Nature of Faith (4:18-25)

*S*o far in his letter to the Roman church and believers everywhere, Paul has laid out the Good News of justification by grace through faith alone in Christ. But just because he presented it doesn't necessarily mean everyone is going to accept it. Paul is wise enough and practical enough to know that some people will object to his message of salvation through faith. He knows his statements are going to need some proof. Paul therefore lays down a very clear *apologetic* in order to defend his position. The basis of his argument is the Old Testament and the founder of the Jewish nation. Watch how skillfully Paul proves his point.

What's an Apologetic?

An apologetic is a rational defense of the Christian faith. It's not apologizing for your faith. It is always being ready to explain your faith—in a gentle and respectful way—whenever you are asked (1 Peter 3:15-16).

By Faith, Not Works (4:1-8)

To begin his arguments, Paul singles out Abraham, the founder of the Jewish nation. Nobody is more revered in Jewish history than Abraham. God's agreement with him and His promised blessings to him (Genesis 12:1-3) put Abraham in a class by himself. If anybody's works were good enough to satisfy God's righteous requirements, Abe's were. In fact, the Jewish leaders in the first century taught that Abraham had a "surplus of merit" that was available to his descendents. In other words, the works of Abraham were so great, enough was leftover for everybody else.

Abraham and the Big Three

Abraham is considered the founding father of the three great monotheistic religions—Judaism, Christianity, and Islam. All three trace their heritage through Abraham. Whether you are reading the writing of the Old Testament Hebrew prophets, the epistles of New Testament Christians, or the revelations of Muhammad, each religion refers to its patriarch, Abraham, as the friend of God.

So here's Paul's logic: If he can show that Abraham came into a right relationship with God through faith and not by works, then he can prove his case that the rest of us need to be saved by faith as well. To put it another way, Paul can justify his case for justification by faith.

Back to Scripture (4:1-5)

Paul wastes no time in answering this question: Was Abraham saved by works or by faith? Paul goes back to the Scriptures and quotes Genesis 15:6:

> *What does the Scripture say? "Abraham believed God, and it was credited to him as righteousness"* (4:3 NIV).

There's that concept of debit and credit we talked about. Even super-spiritual Abraham, the founder of the Jewish nation, had a sin debt that his good works could not offset. Even Abraham could not earn God's favor. So he accepted God's plan to save him through faith, and it was credited to his life ledger as righteousness when he believed (faith is the same thing as belief or "confident assurance"—see Hebrews 11:1).

Okay, so a really big question needs to be answered here. If Abraham didn't know Jesus, just what was he believing in? If you go back to Genesis 12:3, you see that God promised to bless "all the families of the earth" through Abraham. In his letter to the Galatians, Paul reasoned that Abraham understood the implications of this blessing, which looked forward to a Savior for all humankind. Paul writes, "The Scriptures looked forward to this time when God would accept the Gentiles, too, on the basis of their faith" (Galatians 3:8). Even though Abraham and others like him didn't know the person of

Jesus Christ as we can know Him, they knew that God would someday provide a Savior. They believed that God would provide a way for them to be in a right relationship with Him.

Another Example (4:6-8)

Paul continues his defense of justification by faith by bringing David into the picture. David is right up there with Abraham in significance to the Jews. He's the greatest king of Israel, a man after God's own heart. Was David justified by faith as well? Absolutely! Like Abraham, David had a sin debt he couldn't pay back (and his sins were much more heinous and open than Abraham's, at least from our perspective). But he believed, and God credited righteousness to his life ledger. To prove his point, Paul goes to the Psalms and quotes from David, who wrote: "Yes, what joy for those whose record the LORD has cleared of sin" (Psalm 32:2). David understood justification by faith firsthand.

How about you? If you have accepted Jesus as your Savior and Lord, do you understand that you contributed nothing to your salvation except for your deliberate act of faith? If you are still evaluating a personal relationship with God, are you holding back because you don't think you are good enough to be accepted by God? Don't put your faith in your ability to settle your own accounts. Trust in what God has already done by sending Jesus to clear your sin debt.

By Faith, Not Ritual (4:9-12)

Paul goes back to the ritual of circumcision to answer another objection his audience probably had: If Abraham and his descendents, including David, were set apart by God by the Jewish ritual of circumcision, then how can

Paul argue that justification by faith is available to both Jews (the circumcised) and Gentiles (the uncircumcised)? Paul's answer couldn't be any clearer. God accepted (or justified) Abraham first, and Abraham was circumcised later (4:10).

If anything, the circumcision was "a sign that Abraham already had faith and that God had already accepted him and declared him to be righteous—even before he was circumcised" (4:11). Although the ritual pointed to God's work of saving Abraham by faith, it contributed nothing to his status before God.

So what does this mean to us today? Do we have rituals that are signs of our faith relationship with God? How about baptism? The ritual of baptism is a sign that you identify with Christ in His death, burial, and resurrection. It signifies that you have been saved by faith in Christ. However, baptism does not save you any more than circumcision saved Abraham. As R.C. Sproul writes, "The power of baptism is not in the water but in the power of God."

By Faith, Not the Law (4:13-17)

Paul has used his apologetic skills to go after two issues that were very important to the Jews: works and ritual. Now Paul goes after one more sacred cow: God's law, sometimes referred to as the Mosaic law (because it was given by God to Moses).

The Jews considered the Mosaic law, which was a special revelation of God's standards for human conduct, to be the basis for a right relationship with God. If they kept the law, they reasoned, then they were good enough in God's sight. Paul says that if this is true, then "faith is useless" (4:14). Furthermore, the promises given to Abraham would also have to be based on the law. And if that's the case, then the promises are useless. Why? For one very simple reason. "The law brings punishment on those who try to obey it" (4:15). What Paul is saying is this: No one can keep the law in it's entirety, so God's wrath comes down on all people because all people disobey God's law.

"So that's why faith is the key!" writes Paul emphatically (4:16). We can't earn God's promise of eternal life. It's His free gift, accessible and available to anyone who exercises faith in God's ability and plan to save them.

Accessing God's Promise

When we base our relationship with God on ourselves—our works and our ability to live up to God's perfect standards—God's promise of eternal life is worthless to us. When we accept God's gracious gift of salvation by faith, God's promise is assured because our relationship with Him is based on Christ.

The Nature of Faith (4:18-25)

In the final section of this chapter, Paul takes a closer look at faith by focusing on a specific event in Abraham's life that related directly to one of God's promises to him:

Your descendents will be as numerous as the stars (4:18).

Great promise. Only one problem. Abraham and his wife Sarah didn't have any kids, and their prospects were very dim. From a human perspective (that would be *works*), the promise "seemed utterly impossible" (4:18).

That's because both Abraham and Sarah were too old to have kids. (You can read the whole story for yourself in Genesis 17:15–18:15.)

Rather than waver in his belief, Abraham planted his faith in God and His ability to make the promise happen (4:20). "That's not to say that he ignored the facts," writes R.C. Sproul. "But he focused on the bigger fact— that it was God who had promised that he would have a son." Because Abraham had faith in the mighty power of God, he was "absolutely convinced" that God would deliver on every promise (4:21).

Faith in God, Not in Faith

Do you have this kind of faith? Are you absolutely convinced that God will live up to His word? If you aren't, maybe you don't know God well enough, or perhaps you are putting your faith in your faith. That's right—you could be putting your faith in your own ability to believe, thinking that if you believe hard enough or sincerely enough, God will be obligated to answer your prayers. Don't put your faith in your faith. Put your faith in God. Receive His promises and believe them on the basis of who God is and what He has done.

What Is Faith?

The writer of Hebrews summed it up this way: "What is faith? It is the confident assurance that what we hope for is going to happen. It is the evidence of things we cannot yet see" (Hebrews 11:1). R.C. Sproul writes this about faith: "It is simply taking God at His word, believing that He will do what He has promised."

Summing It All Up

Martin Luther said this about Romans 4:23-25: "In these verses the whole of Christ is comprehended." Here Paul summarizes everything he has been talking about so far. This "wonderful truth" of justification by grace through faith is for all people who believe that...

- Jesus died for our sins.
- He was buried.
- He rose again to make us right with God.

■ ▨ ▨

Study the Word

1. Read 1 Peter 3:15-16. Why must we know how to articulate our faith? What is the implication of the phrase, "be ready to explain it" (NLT) or "be prepared to give an answer to everyone who asks you" (NIV)? What does explaining your faith "in a gentle and respectful way" mean?

2. Do you think most people believe we are born with a debit on the sin side of our "life ledger," a credit on the righteousness side, or a zero balance on both sides? What are the implications of each viewpoint?

3. Read the story of Abraham and Isaac in Genesis 22:1-19. How did this incident prepare Abraham to look forward to a Savior?

4. This chapter talked about baptism as a ritual that is a sign of our faith relationship with God. Do you participate in other rituals that do the same thing? What is the significance of each one?

5. Why does every other major religion feature works as a way to achieve salvation or ultimate happiness? Why do you think Christianity stands alone as the

only belief system that features salvation by grace through faith alone?

Which way of life—one built on works or one built on faith—is ultimately more satisfying? Why?

6. Describe a situation where someone might have faith in faith. What's the downside of doing this?

7. Read Romans 4:23-25 and 1 Corinthians 15:3-4. List the parallels between these two great passages of Scripture.

Really Saved

In Romans 3–4, Paul presented some very convincing arguments that demonstrate our need for a Savior. He has shown how that Savior, Jesus Christ, paid our insurmountable sin debt by dying in our place. All we need to do is accept by faith what Christ has already done. We can do nothing to aid in the process because salvation is a free gift from God. Now, in the next four chapters of Romans, Paul is going to show us the nature and the effect of our salvation, coming to a glorious conclusion in Romans 8:38-39.

Starting in Romans 5, the subject of this chapter, Paul begins to develop this theme by giving us several benefits of justification through faith, beginning with a big one: We have peace with God. And it isn't just a temporary peace. This is for keeps. Our salvation is secure—nothing and no one can ever take it away.

If you have ever wondered whether or not you are really saved—if you want assurance that your salvation is real—then this chapter and the ones to follow are talking right to you.

Chapter 5

Peace with God

Romans 5

*W*hat's *A*head

- ☐ Benefits of Justification (5:1-5)
- ☐ Friends with God (5:6-11)
- ☐ Adam and Christ (5:12-21)

*H*ave you ever heard the expression, "sue for peace"? We mostly associate the word *sue* with trying to get something from someone else, but another definition has to do with making a humble, earnest request for something. It literally means begging for mercy. In military terms, the phrase refers to a conquered nation suing the conquering nation for peace, thereby ending hostilities.

As Paul begins Romans 5, keep that image in your mind. In our culture, everyone wants something from someone else. People even want something from God (no doubt some people would love to sue God because they think He's responsible for their sorry lives). But that's the wrong attitude. We need to humbly and earnestly ask God for forgiveness. We need to beg for His mercy and accept His offer of salvation. We need to sue God for peace. If we do, He will give us His peace and a whole lot more.

Benefits of Justification (5:1-5)

Paul begins Romans 5 with the word *Therefore,* signifying a summary of all that he's said previously. His summary includes the wonderful benefits that come to those who have been justified through faith.

Peace with God (5:1)

The Bible often talks about the peace of God, and when it does we usually think about our own sense of personal peace. But that's not what Paul is talking about here. When we are hopeless and helpless in our sin, we are literally God's enemies. In a spiritual sense, we are at war with God. When we surrender to Jesus and accept what He has done for us, we literally "sue for peace." God graciously ends the hostilities between us—but that's not all. According to Douglas Moo, the peace Paul is talking about carries with it the idea of the well-being and the prosperity of the believer. God doesn't just call a truce. He lavishes His blessings on us.

Access to God (5:2)

Because of our new life in Christ, we have not only peace with God but also access to the very presence of God. William Barclay writes that this word *access* carries two meanings. First, it pictures our entry into the presence of royalty. Think of it! Christ ushers us into the presence of God. We were once His enemies, but now we can stand before Him without shame.

Second, we have access to the shelter of God's grace. Barclay writes that the picture is of a ship coming into a harbor, safe from the waves and storms. Once we struggled in the open sea of sin, but now we can rest in God's forgiveness because we have anchored our ship in the harbor of His grace.

> So let us come boldly to the throne of our gracious God. There we will receive his mercy, and we will find grace to help us when we need it.
>
> Hebrews 4:16

Joy in Suffering (5:2-5)

Not many people would see the theme of these verses as a benefit. What? You mean we have to suffer? Yes we do. One of the biggest misconceptions people have about the Christian life is that you will be happy once you turn your life over to God. Where does the Bible say, "For God so loved the world, that he gave His only Son, so that everyone who believes in Him will be happy"? Scripture contains no such verse and no such promise. Our assurance is that we are saved from God's wrath (5:9), and we are guaranteed eternal life with God (John 3:16). Happiness is never part of the deal.

If anything, we are guaranteed a life filled with trials and troubles. So what's the benefit in that? Paul writes that we can rejoice in our suffering, our problems, and our trials because our troubles teach us patience and perseverance. This in turn builds up our character, and our character leads to hope, or "our confident expectation of salvation" (5:4). The meaning of this confident expectation is two-pronged. First, your salvation in this life is completely effective. You don't have to wonder, *Am I really saved?* If you have acknowledged your sinful state and your need for a Savior, and if you have accepted

Jesus Christ as your Savior, then your salvation is effective because it is based on God's work, not yours.

Second, your salvation is completely secure. Paul writes, "And this expectation will not disappoint us" (5:5). The word *disappoint* literally means, "put to shame." According to Douglas Moo, the word is also used in the Old Testament to mean, "suffer judgment." In other words, your salvation—your hope—gives you such a standing before God that when Judgment Day comes, you will not be put to shame. You will not suffer judgment. The work that God has done in Christ for you now will still be in effect in eternity. That's what people mean when they use the term *eternal security.*

> When a man's hope is in God it cannot turn to dust and ashes. When a man's hope is in God it cannot be disappointed. When a man's hope is in the love of God it can never be an illusion, for God is loving us with an everlasting love, which is backed by an everlasting power.
>
> —*William Barclay*

Friends with God (5:6-11)

After giving us the benefits of justification, Paul reminds us just how much we were in debt because of sin.

Helpless and Hopeless (5:6-8)

When we think about where we were before we received God's gift of salvation and the benefits that go along with it, we should fall on our knees in thanks to God. We were utterly helpless in our own sin. We deserved nothing but God's wrath and judgment. Yet it was exactly at that time—"at just the right time"—that Christ came to earth and died for us. And we weren't just sinners; we were God's enemies. Jesus didn't die for His friends; He died for His enemies. You can't even measure a love like that.

From Enemies to Friends (5:9-11)

When we are reconciled to God, we are literally restored to friendship with God. This has two distinct benefits:

- *We will be saved from God's wrath in the future.* This benefit alone is worth the price of admission. When all people are judged, those God calls friends will be spared eternal punishment.

- *We can enjoy our relationship with God in the present.* As friends with God, we can enjoy His presence and blessings the instant we put our faith in Jesus Christ.

Adam and Christ (5:12-21)

This last section of Romans 5 could take up an entire chapter of this Bible study, but we're only going to hit the highlights. You can dig deeper on your own or in your group. Here's the crucial question to consider as you study this section: How could the sin of just one person impact the entire human race from that day forward?

Good question! Why should you be responsible for something your great-great-great-great (etc., etc.) grandfather did? The answer to that question goes to the heart of another LTW: *imputation.* Let's look at what this means.

Adam Is Our Representative (5:12-14)

Here's how John Phillips explains imputation and the problem of sin:

Adam, by the fall, introduced to his race, as yet unborn, the deadly virus of sin. We are not sinners because we sin; we sin because we are sinners. And because we sinned in Adam, death is imputed to us.

Unger's Bible Dictionary defines *imputation* this way: "to count over unto one's account." That's the sin on the left side of your life ledger. Every person born since Adam has inherited a sin debt from him. Each of us is born with a negative balance. Therefore, *we aren't sinners because we sin.* If that were the case, then we would be born with the capacity *not* to sin, but we're not. Instead, *we sin because we are sinners.* We can't help but sin. It's in our nature.

But how is that possible? And is it fair? We went to Wayne Grudem's *Systematic Theology* for some answers. First, a few thoughts about God and sin:

- God is not responsible for sin (Deuteronomy 32:4), nor is He surprised by sin.

- Sin was present in the angelic world before Adam and Eve.

- No negative or evil force in the world is equal to God. The holy and transcendent God rules over all and will triumph over all.

The reason we inherit Adam's sin and guilt is that Adam was the God-appointed representative of the entire human race. Just like voters elect people to represent them at various levels of government, God elected Adam to represent us (and His vote counts for a whole lot). Under this system of representation, when Adam

sinned, God saw all those who would descend from
Adam as sinners. He imputed—or counted—Adam's sin
to us.

Would I Have Chosen Differently?

You may wonder what you would have done had you been in
Adam's place. Adam clearly made a foolish choice—so foolish
that any right-thinking person would have chosen differently.
Does that let us off the hook? Grudem explains that we voluntarily commit sins apart from our inherited guilt, and this will
ultimately be the basis of our judgment on Judgment Day. Paul
doesn't say, "We will be judged because of Adam's sin." He
writes, "God will judge all people according to what they have
done" (2:6). Ultimately, we have to trust God in this. Grudem
writes: "God counted Adam's guilt as belonging to us, and
since God is the ultimate judge of all things in the universe,
and since his thoughts are always true, Adam's guilt does in
fact belong to us."

Christ Is Our Representative (5:15-19)

Another reason for accepting God's decision to
appoint Adam as our representative is that God also
appointed Christ to be our representative. If you think
being represented by Adam is unfair, then perhaps you
should think the same about being represented by
Christ. Paul draws several parallels between Adam and
Christ in four remarkable verses:

- Just as Adam's sin was imputed to the entire
  human race, Christ's righteousness was imputed
  to those who believe in Him.

- Adam's sin brought us sin, condemnation, and
  death. But the righteousness of Christ brought

those who receive Him by faith forgiveness, acceptance, and eternal life.

- Just as Adam's sin affected us even before we were born, Christ's work on the cross affected us before we were born (5:8).

Grace Greater than Our Sin (5:20-21)

One of the great values of God's law is that it shows us how sinful we are. The law doesn't *cause* people to sin. People sinned even before the law was given (5:13). But the law, which is a reflection of God's perfect standard, declares us guilty. It shows us how far from perfect we really are.

Rather than leave us dead in our sins, God poured His grace upon us in a way far greater than our sin. Paul writes: "As people sinned more and more, God's wonderful kindness became even more abundant" (5:20). We were once slaves to sin, but by grace God has freed us so that we have peace with Him and eternal life through Jesus Christ His Son.

*A*mazing *G*race

John Newton, an eighteenth-century slave owner with a reputation for profanity and debauchery, was transformed by God's grace. Though his own wretchedness was profound, God's grace was greater. Newton was converted, and in 1779 he composed what is perhaps the most famous of all hymns:

Amazing grace, how sweet the sound, that saved a wretch like me!

I once was lost but now am found, was blind but now I see.

That same year Newton became the rector of a church in London, where he ministered to the poor and wealthy alike.

One of his parishioners was an influential member of Parliament by the name of William Wilberforce, who was strongly influenced by Newton's thoughts on the African slave trade. Wilberforce became a prime mover in the abolition of slavery in England.

■ ■ ■

$\mathcal{S}$tudy the $\mathcal{W}$ord

1. What are the main roadblocks to peace in the world today? Answer this on two levels: external peace and internal peace. When are you most at peace?

2. Are Christians ever guilty of presenting the Good News message as a way to be happy rather than as a way to be made right with a wrathful God? Why do we do this?

   What happens when someone says yes to Christ because they believe He will make them happy? What's the downside of this?

3. One of the biggest anxieties Christians have is over the matter of eternal security. Why do you think Christians struggle with this so much? Have you ever had questions about your salvation? What did you do about it?

What would you tell someone who asks you, "How do I know I'm saved?"

4. Read James 1:2-4 and 1 Peter 1:6-7. List three benefits to suffering as a Christian. Talk about the last trial you went through. What did you learn from it?

5. Four different times in Romans 5 (NIV), Paul uses the phrase "how much more." Draw a chart that lists and compares two things: 1) What Paul was describing in each case, and 2) what each one means for us on a practical level.

6. Why shouldn't we believe that we would have chosen differently had we been in Adam's bare feet?

7. Do you think God set up Adam and Eve so they had no choice but to sin? Why or why not?

What would have happened if God had created Adam unable to sin? Would the human race have enjoyed a better relationship with God?

Looking for Loopholes?

Looking for loopholes is part of human nature. Lawyers are especially good at this (just ask Bruce). Show them a law, and they'll look for a loophole. But don't come down too hard on lawyers. Even those of us not trained in the law will look for ways to get around something, especially if it infringes on our freedom or what we perceive to be our rights.

At the end of Romans 5, Paul makes a statement that invites loophole lookers. He writes, "God's law was given so that all people could see how sinful they were. But as people sinned more and more, God's wonderful kindness became more abundant" (5:20). He seems to be saying, "Sin makes God look good." In fact, some people in Paul's day believed just that, so for them the loophole was simple: If sin causes God's grace to increase, what's so bad about sinning?

Today we might express the loophole this way: As long as God keeps forgiving, we can keep on sinning. Is that what Paul meant to say? If not, can He close the loophole? You're about to find out.

Chapter 6

Freedom in Christ

Romans 6

*W*hat's *A*head

- United with Christ (6:1-14)

- Slaves to God (6:15-23)

*W*e can learn a lot about the art of argument from the apostle Paul. We're not talking about the kind of argument where two people shout at each other without listening (that's what politics is for). We're referring to a classic give-and-take discussion where the facts are presented in a logical manner to make a case.

A smart arguer will anticipate the objections, conclusions, and misinterpretations of others. In other words, he will find the loopholes first—and close them. That's exactly what Paul does in Romans 6. After stating that more sin makes God's grace increase, he states two potential loopholes in the form of two questions:

1. "Should we keep on sinning so that God can show us more and more kindness and forgiveness?" (6:1).

2. "So since God's grace has set us free from the law, does this mean we can go on sinning?" (6:15).

Now, you may look at these two loopholes and say, "Who would think that?" Don't kid yourself. We've all asked those questions, especially the second one. We've all figured that we can outsmart God on this issue of sin (like that's really going to happen), so we continue to sin even though we know it's wrong. As you study Romans 6, you will see that Paul's goal is to deal with these two misguided tendencies.

United with Christ (6:1-14)

In the first half of the chapter, Paul addresses the first question, which basically deals with the idea that justification by grace through faith without works encourages people to sin. Paul answers this question with a resounding, "You can't be serious!" Actually, he writes, "Of course not!" (NLT) and "By no means!" (NIV). And then he sets out to prove his case by using the metaphor of baptism to show that we have died to sin.

Free Grace and Sin

Some people have actually taught that the doctrine of free grace puts a value on sin. They believe grace allows them to sin all they want now and still retain their standing in eternity. These teachers are called *antinomians* because they are against *(anti)* the moral law *(nomos)*. This is the opposite of someone who believes that works will get you into heaven. Both extremes are wrong. Theologian John Gerstner writes: "The Christian religion, while it preaches pure grace, unadulterated grace with no meritorious contribution from us whatsoever, at the same time requires of us the loftiest conceivable conduct."

Dead to Sin (6:1-2)

Here is a fundamental truth about sin every l needs to know: When we receive Christ through faith, we die to sin. This doesn't mean we no longer have the capacity to sin. It means that in principle, sin is like a dead body in the life of a believer. Sin has no more power than a corpse. How does this happen? When Christ died on the cross, He took on not only the guilt and consequences of our sins but also our sinful nature itself. Paul writes, "Our old sinful selves were crucified with Christ so that sin might lose its power in our lives" (6:6). In other words, the old sin nature we inherited from Adam has been put to death.

One way the Roman government would punish a murderer was to tie the body of the dead victim onto his back, forcing him to walk around with a rotting corpse. Can you imagine the stench and the horror? Well, try imagining because that's what life is like for a believer who sins. We strap on that dead, rotting body of sin and haul it around.

Buried with Christ (6:3-4)

Just as we were represented by Adam in his sin, we are represented by Christ in His death, burial, and resurrection. Paul uses the concept of baptism to make his point. The word *baptized* here does not refer to baptism by water. That certainly is one meaning of the word, and clearly the Roman believers were familiar with the symbolism of water baptism (see the box on the next page), but *baptism* has another meaning that is more relevant here. It's the idea of one person *identifying* with another.

Picture a piece of white cloth and a bowl of red dye. When you dip—or *baptize*—the cloth into the dye, it takes on the color of the dye. Its identity changes. That's what happens when you become a Christian. You identify with Christ. In effect, you change your colors.

Just as Jesus died for our sins, was buried, and was raised from the dead, we have died to sin, have been buried with Christ, and have been raised back to life with Him. We are no longer the same people. We have identified with Christ, and we can't go back to the way we were any more than the dyed cloth can go back to its original color.

_B_aptism and the _B_eliever

When Paul used the metaphor of baptism to describe the new life of the believer, first-century Christians knew exactly what he was talking about. They saw water baptism as a symbol of their faith. When people confessed Christ as Savior, they "followed Christ into baptism." Baptism was symbolic of dying and rising again. When new believers descended into the water, they were figuratively being buried in the grave, and when they came out of the water, they were rising from the dead. They "died to the old life of sin and rose to the new life of grace," writes Barclay.

Raised with Christ (6:5-11)

Jesus proved His power over death when He rose from the dead. The resurrection of Christ is such an important part of our faith that without it we have no faith. In his first letter to the Corinthians Paul writes, "And if Christ has not been raised, then your faith is useless, and you are still under condemnation for your sins" (1 Corinthians 15:17). But Christ did rise from the dead. It's a historical, provable fact. Because Christ conquered death, we are no longer slaves to sin. As we said, this doesn't mean that sin is erased from our lives. We still have the capacity to sin, but the power and principle of sin in our lives is broken for good. R.C. Sproul writes:

> We do not have to obey temptation; we now have the God-given ability to resist it. We are now free, by God's grace, to grow in holiness, sinning less and less while obeying God more and more.

You see, realizing that sin has been defeated in our lives is one thing—a very important thing. But living "for the glory of God through Christ Jesus" (6:11) is quite another. Our *position* is one of freedom from sin's grip. But our *practice* should be living every day as if that is true. Our constant desire and goal should be to know and glorify God and to be in submission to His will for us.

Don't Let Sin Control You (6:12-14)

Before you were a Christian, you only had one way to live—under the control of the old sin nature. You had no choice in the matter because the "old man" of sin was still alive in you. As a Christian, the old man is dead and no longer has mastery over you. However, you still have the capacity to sin. You have a choice. You can...

- let sin control the way you live (6:12)
- let your body become a tool of wickedness (6:13)

Or you can...

- give yourself completely to God (6:13)
- use your whole body as a tool to do what is right for the glory of God (6:13)

The choice is yours. Obviously, it's not a tough choice, at least not in *principle*. Where it's tough is in *practice*, especially if you're looking for God's forgiveness and grace as a loophole. Don't fall into that trap! Realize that "sin is no longer your master" (6:14). Wake up to the fact that you are dead to sin and alive to God. Instead of giving yourself to sin, give yourself to God.

---

*S*anctification and the *C*hristian

The LTW for this process of identifying with the death and resurrection of Christ is *sanctification*. It's a process that continues throughout our Christian lives by which God moves us further and further from the ruling power and love of sin. Wayne Grudem writes: "The role we play in sanctification is both a *passive* one in which we depend on God to sanctify us, and an *active* one in which we strive to obey God and take steps that will increase our sanctification."

Slaves to God (6:15-23)

In the first half of Romans 6, Paul used the metaphor of baptism to answer the question, "Should we keep on sinning *so that* grace may increase?" Now in the second half, he asks the question, "Should we keep on sinning *because* we are under grace?" Again, he answers, "Of course not!" and then he supports his response by using the metaphor of slavery, something people in the first century were very familiar with.

Born a Slave (6:15-19)

Slavery is an ugly word and rightfully so. The idea of human beings being treated as property to be bought and sold is repulsive. It goes against our sense of freedom.

Sorry to burst your idealistic bubble, but no one is absolutely free. No matter who you are—rich or poor, male or female, young or old—you have to serve something or somebody. The question is not, "How do I become free?" but "Whom or what am I going to serve?" In the spiritual realm—the one that counts for eternity—you have two choices. Paul lays them out this way in 6:16:

- You can choose sin, which leads to death.

- You can choose to obey God and receive His approval.

Because of our sin nature, all of us are born as slaves to sin, but we aren't forced to stay that way. Every person chooses to stay a slave of sin or to become a slave of God. Getting the facts straight is important when making your decision. Just what are the potential upsides and downsides of each choice? The "slave to sin" side doesn't seem to have much of an upside. Earlier in Romans, Paul describes the life of sin as a downward spiral that leads to more sin (1:24). By contrast, someone who is a slave to God is in an upward spiral of righteousness that leads to holiness (5:3-4). That's the idea here in Romans 6. Because of Christ, we have been set free from sin and have become slaves to our new master, righteousness (6:18).

For the Christian, being a slave to righteousness is a matter of obedience. According to Stott, obedience "is the very essence of slavery." Conversion is an act of self-surrender," he writes. "Self-surrender leads to slavery; and slavery demands a total, radical, exclusive obedience."

Here is the natural progression for people who choose to obey God:

1. They used to be slaves to sin (6:17).

'hey obeyed the new teaching with all their heart (6:17).

3. They have been set free from sin (6:18).

4. They have become slaves to righteousness (6:18).

𝒜 𝒲ord on 𝒮lavery

If you are uncomfortable with all this slave talk, perhaps a little background on slavery in the first century will be helpful. The Romans were very familiar with slavery. Nearly one in four of the inhabitants of Rome and the Italian peninsula were slaves, and the Roman Empire needed more than a half million new slaves annually. However, slaves were not treated in quite the same barbaric manner as they have been in other slave-holding societies. Howard Vos writes that a Roman slave had no identifying mark of ownership, which meant that you couldn't tell the difference between a slave and a free man on the streets. Enterprising slaves had some financial benefits, and slaves could be freed in Rome without a lot of red tape (slaves could even buy their freedom). As a result, many people volunteered to be slaves because they received security and a wage they wouldn't otherwise have.

Free from the Power of Sin (6:20-23)

One of the biggest misconceptions people have about Christianity is that becoming a Christian obligates you to a set of regulations and restrictions. People think that once they surrender their life to Christ, they will lose their freedom. Don't you think that's why many people resist the message of the Gospel? What a lie! People are so blinded to their enslavement to their own sin that they can't see the truth of what true freedom is. If only they knew that real freedom comes when Christ sets us

free from the power of sin. Real freedom and true fulfill-
ment come when we voluntarily become slaves of God
and "do those things that lead to holiness and result in
eternal life" (6:22).

How do we get this message across? First, our hearts
need to break for the lost. We need to read the last verse in
this chapter and think about where our friends and family
members who are enslaved to sin will spend eternity.

*For the wages of sin is death, but the free gift of
God is eternal life through Jesus Christ our Lord.*

Thank God today for the free gift of eternal life that
you have accepted. Then ask Him to break your heart for
those who are paying the wages of sin.

◻ ◻ ◻

Study the Word

1. Why do some Christians think continuing to sin is
   perfectly harmless?

2. Read James 2:14-20 and then respond to this statement: We are justified by faith alone, but we are not
   justified by a faith that is alone.

3. In what way is baptism both a funeral and a resurrection for the believer?

4. Compare Romans 6:5-11 and 1 Corinthians 15:17-20. What kind of faith would we have if Christ had not been raised from the dead? With this in mind, do you need to know for sure that the resurrection of Christ actually took place? How do you know?

5. Why must our *position* as people free from sin line up with our *practice* of living as if that is true? What kind of signal does the world receive when those two things are not aligned?

6. According to R.C. Sproul, Paul argues in Romans 6 that a person who is truly saved cannot continue in a lifestyle of "casual sin." This brings up a sticky issue. What if a Christian continues in a lifestyle of sin? Does that mean that person has lost his or her salvation? Was the person never saved in the first place? See Hebrews 10:26-31.

7. How does slavery to God differ from slavery to sin?

8. Has this chapter helped you in your struggle with sin? How?

Morality Can't Save Us

A well-known verse from the book of Proverbs says, "Pride goes before destruction, and haughtiness before a fall" (Proverbs 16:18). Pride can take many forms, but one of the most blatant is in the area of morality. Some people love to set themselves up as paragons of virtue and morality while criticizing those who don't meet their standards. But most people like this have a problem: They can't live up to the standards they set for others. This is not always the case, of course, but consider these people:

- the evangelist who preached against adultery and then got caught with a prostitute

- the high-profile moralist who wrote a best-selling book about virtues and then had to admit he was a high-stakes gambler

- the football coach who demanded exemplary behavior from his players while he was visiting strip clubs

We shouldn't condemn people like this (remember all of that "he who is without sin cast the first stone" business that Jesus talked about?), but we should learn a lesson about the nature of morality and the law. In Romans 7, Paul warns that morality and the law in themselves can't save us. If anything, the law incites rebellion. Does that mean that the law is faulty, or that living a morally upright life is impossible? Not at all. In fact, God expects us to live as holy and righteous people. We just need help from another source in order to do what He wants us to do.

Chapter 7

Struggling with Sin

Romans 7

---

*W*hat's *A*head

- [ ] Released from the Law (7:1-6)
- [ ] The Value of the Law (7:7-13)
- [ ] The Christian's Great Struggle (7:14-25)

*O*ne of the great benefits of doing a study like this on an entire book of the Bible is that you get to see the whole picture. We are often tempted to come to conclusions based on a study of a few verses or even a chapter or two. All Scripture is valuable, but the best way to study the Bible is to always read in context: a word or phrase in the context of a verse, a verse in the context of a chapter, a chapter in the context of a book, a book in the context of a Testament, and a Testament in the context of the Bible (theologians call this the "concentric circles of context").

A case in point is Romans 7. This well-known chapter—with the famous verse, "What a wretched man I am! Who will rescue me from this body of death?"

(7:24 NIV)—can stand alone, but it makes much more sense when you read it in the context of the chapters that come before and after it. As you're going to see, Paul's arguments about the law and sin are a little hard to follow. However, when you link this chapter to Romans 6 (which tells us that the power of sin is broken) and Romans 8 (which tells us how to live a life controlled by the Holy Spirit), Romans 7 is much easier to understand and apply.

Released from the Law (7:1-6)

After giving an illustration from slavery (6:15-23), Paul picks up where he left off in 6:14. He describes freedom from the law by virtue of God's grace. In these first six verses he tells us how the law works and why it should no longer have power over us.

The real issue of this chapter—and it's a biggie—is one we all face on a daily basis. Knowing that we have died to sin because we are united in Christ (6:2-3) is one thing; dealing with the sin nature that's still in us is an entirely different matter. This is the inner struggle that every believer faces. We should wrestle with this conflict because God hasn't let us off the hook just because the law no longer has power over us. He isn't saying to us, "If sin still has a hold on you, that's okay. Just do the best you can." If anything, God has raised the bar. He doesn't just want us to not sin. God wants us to proactively "do those things that lead to holiness" (6:22).

An Illustration from Marriage (7:1-3)

Starting in 7:7, Paul is going to show us the relationship of the law to sin. It plays a big part, as you're going to see. But first he wants to show us the law's relationship

to us, because ultimately that will help us better understand our relationship to sin.

To help us understand the law's relationship to every
believer, Paul uses a very clever analogy drawn from
marriage. If you're not married, go along with us here (if
it's any consolation, Paul wasn't married either). If you
are married, don't get any ideas about bumping off your
spouse.

Here's how the analogy works. The wife is the believer
and the husband is the law. Just as a wife is no longer
obligated to her husband after he dies, the believer is no
longer obligated to the written code of the law because
Christ died. As long as her husband is alive, the wife is
obligated to stay married to him. The law of marriage
has power over her. But death can set her free from that
law, allowing her to enter into a new relationship.

Producing Good Fruit (7:4)

In the same way, the death of Christ sets us free from
the written law, allowing us to enter into a new relationship with Christ, who fulfilled the law perfectly.
Only then are we able to "do those things that lead to
holiness," which Paul now refers to as "good fruit, that
is, good deeds for God."

We Are the Bride of Christ

In other letters, Paul uses this analogy of the wife and the husband and marriage to describe the relationship between
believers and Jesus Christ. All believers—collectively known
as the church—are the bride, and Christ is the bridegroom
(2 Corinthians 11:2; Ephesians 5:25-26).

A New Kind of Law (7:5-6)

The law isn't useless or bad. God's law is simply a standard—a perfect standard—that no human being can possibly meet. But Christ was able to meet the standard. He lived a perfect life, and then He died for us so the power of the law and sin over us was broken, releasing us to "really serve God, not in the old way by obeying the letter of the law, but in the new way, by the Spirit" (7:6).

God's law, representing His perfect requirements, doesn't go away or change, but the way we meet those requirements does change. We no longer have to live up to God's written requirements. Instead, we are called to live up to God's righteous requirements "in the new way, by the Spirit" (7:6). Here's how R.C. Sproul puts it:

> Having been "married" to Christ, we now are able to keep the law, for He gives us His Holy Spirit to enable us to obey God's righteous requirements. The law no longer condemns us but instead guides us in the way God would have us live.

The Value of the Law (7:7-13)

In order to clear up any misconceptions his readers might have about the law, Paul asks yet another rhetorical question: "Well then, am I suggesting that the law of God is evil?" (7:7). And he answers the question just like he did in 6:2 and 6:15—"Of course not!" So what is the law good for? Maybe an illustration will help.

---

*I*t's the *L*aw

Imagine you are driving down a lonely road in Nevada. No other car or truck is in sight. You haven't seen any speed limit sign, so you gradually increase your speed until you are cruising comfortably along at 90 mph. Then you pass a sign that clearly says Speed Limit 70, and you realize something very important: You are breaking the law. But do you slow down? Maybe a little, but you conclude that the law is stupid, so you don't meet its exact requirements. You are still speeding.

In fact, you are tempted to go even faster as you mutter to yourself, "If that sign weren't there, I could go as fast as I want." You even get mad at the sign, but is the sign at fault? No, the sign is simply the messenger. It's telling you the standard for speed set by the legislature. Even if the sign were not posted, you would still be a lawbreaker.

The Law Shows Us Our Sin (7:7-8)

In the same way that the speed limit sign is not the cause of your speeding, the law is not the cause of the act of sin. Our sin nature is the cause (remember, we sin because we are sinners, not the other way around). That's what Paul means when he says, "But sin took advantage of this law" (7:8).

$\mathcal{P}$aul in the $\mathcal{F}$irst $\mathcal{P}$erson

You will notice in this section that Paul switches from the second to the first person. Instead of referring to "you," he begins to use "I." Is he referring to himself as an individual who struggles with sin, or is he using himself as an example for the entire human race? He probably has both references in mind. Before he was converted, Paul wasn't fully aware of just how sinful he was, but once he was confronted with his own sin and his need for a Savior, he became acutely aware of his sinful nature. At the same time, Paul shares a common nature with all of us. When he uses his "I," we know exactly what he's talking about.

When Paul is talking about sin here, he isn't referring to a particular act of sin but to the principle of sin. Sin is a part of our natures always lurking below the surface. When the law pops up—like the speed limit sign—it reminds us we are sinners. It can even stimulate us to more sin. But the law is never the cause of our sin.

The Law Shows Us Who We Really Are (7:9-12)

"Ignorance of the law is no excuse." That's how any judge would respond to anyone who said, "But I didn't know I was breaking the law." People may think being blissfully ignorant of God's perfect standards is okay, but that's not going to cut it on Judgment Day. A time comes in every person's life when he or she learns the truth about right and wrong and realizes that the wages of sin is death (6:23).

Again, the law is not the problem. Sin is the problem. The law is holy, right, and good (7:12):

- *holy* because it comes from a holy God
- *right* because it forbids and condemns sin
- *good* because it shows us the way of life

The Law Condemns Us (7:13)

Even though sin—not the law—leads to death, the law gets blamed. In our own culture, the death penalty has become the bad guy in the debate. To many people, the sin isn't what's evil, the law is. But that's backward. The law doesn't cause the crime, the lawbreaker does.

The Christian's Great Struggle (7:14-25)

"The trouble is not with the law, but with me...I am a slave to sin." That is Paul's conclusion in the final section, and it's our conclusion too.

The Problem Defined (4:14-17)

The root of the problem is simple. The law is good, but we still have a sinful nature. Although we have died to the law with Christ, sin is still a force to be reckoned with. Instead of doing what is right, we do the things we hate. This is the great struggle of the believer.

Can you identify with this? If you can, that's a good thing. Knowing you were sinning and not feeling bad about it would be a terrible thing. The fact that you are fighting daily to obey God shows that you are one of God's own children. As R.C. Sproul writes, if you did not fight to obey God, you would not be saved.

Unable to Do Right (7:18-24)

Throughout this chapter Paul has been talking about the Mosaic law (also known as God's law), which God gave us to show us His perfect standard. Now Paul is talking about "another law at work within me that is at war with my mind" (7:23). This law is the principle of sin. *The Bible Knowledge Commentary* refers to this as "the reality of ever present evil in an individual when he wants to do good."

Paul deliberately uses the word *war*. Truly we are involved in a serious battle between the good we want to do and the sin we keep committing. As long as we try to win the battle in our own strength, the sin principle will win every time, leaving us "wretched" (NIV) and "miserable" (NLT). But believers don't have to live this way. We can win the battle!

The Answer Is in Christ (7:25)

Now we come to one of the most encouraging verses in all of Scripture. R.C. Sproul tells us why.

- We know that we have died to sin because Christ paid our *penalty* in the *past.*

- The effect of this is that we have been freed from sin's *power* in the *present.*

- What we need is the assurance that we will be free from sin's *presence* in the *future.*

We can take comfort. We can say with Paul, "Thank God! The answer is in Jesus Christ our Lord." A day will come when sin and death will be defeated once and for all because Jesus will come again to make all things right.

▨ ▨ ▨

Study the Word

1. Why must we always read Scripture in context?

2. Why do Christians still struggle with temptation and sin? Are certain situations more difficult for you to deal with than others? What do you do when these situations come up?

3. Why does the law—either the law of God or the laws of culture—create within us the desire to sin?

4. What's the difference between living up to God's written requirements and living up to His requirement for righteousness? Why is the first scenario impossible and the second one possible?

5. Do you see a trend in our culture to make excuses for breaking the law? Why is saying "I was wrong" so hard? What other words or phrases do people use to describe their sin?

6. Do you think non-Christians struggle with sin as much as Christians do? How does guilt enter into the picture? Is feeling guilty about sin a positive thing? Why or why not?

7. Can you identify with Paul's confession in Romans 7:14-20? In what way is our struggle with sin like a war?

An Amazing Thing

Less than 24 hours before He died on the cross for our sins, Jesus met with His disciples in a place called the Upper Room and told them some amazing things. "I am going to prepare a place for you," He said, giving them a brief description of heaven (John 14:1-4). He reassured them that He was the only way to God when He told them, "No one can come to the Father except through me" (John 14:6).

Jesus also told His disciples that He would soon be leaving them to go back to the Father, but He would not be leaving them alone. "And I will ask the Father, and he will give you another Counselor, who will never leave you," Jesus said. "He is the Holy Spirit, who leads into all truth" (John 14:16-17). The Holy Spirit came seven weeks after Jesus rose from the dead (Acts 2:1-4), and many believers felt His power. But not everyone understood what living in the power of the Holy Spirit meant.

That's what Paul is about to tell his Roman readers, and it's very instructive for us as well. Up to this point Paul has mentioned the Spirit only two times, but in this chapter he will refer to the Holy Spirit nineteen times. He wants to make sure we know what living in the Spirit is all about.

*C*ha

Living in the Spirit

Romans 8

*W*hat's *A*head

- Controlled by the Spirit (8:1-17)
- Suffering Now, Glory Later (8:18-30)
- If God Is for Us (8:31-39)

*T*his chapter is all about living in the Spirit, but it's also about assurance: Once you are truly saved, nothing can separate you from the love of Christ. Paul began talking about assurance in Romans 5. There we learned that Christians who have been justified by faith have full assurance of being saved when Judgment Day comes. After dealing with sin and the law in Romans 6 and 7, Paul comes back to the matter of assurance in Romans 8, but this time he expands the scope of his argument. We are assured of not only a life with Christ in heaven but also a productive and Christ-honoring life here on earth.

Paul is also going to show us how we can experience victory in our struggle with sin. We can't win the battle with sin on our own, but we can through the power God has given us in the Holy Spirit.

Controlled by the Spirit (8:1-17)

If the Bible has a verse all Christians should have mounted on a wall where they can see it every day, it's Romans 8:1. This verse contains the Good News message for everyone who has trusted Jesus Christ for salvation:

> *So now there is no condemnation for those who belong to Christ Jesus.*

Sometimes we take our faith too lightly. We don't realize just how bad off we were before we accepted Christ's saving work on our behalf. Because of our sin, we were

- guilty before a holy God
- condemned to die

A Different Plan (8:1-4)

The law of Moses couldn't save us because none of us could keep the law. But God's plan centered on Jesus, who lived a perfect life and met the law's requirements for us. In the process Christ took on our death penalty and with it the black cloud of condemnation. This is why Jesus came—not to condemn the world (which was already condemned) but to save it (John 3:17).

"*No*" *Means* "*No*"

The word *no*—as in *no condemnation*—means *no*, not just for now, but for all time. John MacArthur writes: "That is the heart and soul of the gospel—that Jesus completely and permanently paid the debt of sin and the penalty of the law (which is condemnation to death) for every person who humbly asks for mercy and trusts in Him."

Two Ways to Live (8:5-13)

Two kinds of people make up the entire population of the world: those who are dominated by their sinful natures and those who are controlled by the Holy Spirit. In this section, Paul clearly contrasts the two.

Those Dominated by the Sinful Nature	*Those Controlled by the Holy Spirit*
Think about sinful things (8:5), which leads to death (8:6)	Think about things that please the Spirit (8:5), which leads to life and peace (8:6)
Are hostile to God (8:7)	Have the Spirit of God living in them (8:9)
Never obey God's laws and never will (8:7)	Though the body will die, their spirit is alive (8:10)
Can never please God (8:8)	Have been made right with God (8:10)
Will perish (8:11)	Will live forever (8:11)

Clearly Paul is contrasting the unsaved person with the Christian. No Christian is completely dominated by a sinful nature. Yes, a Christian still has the ability to sin, and sometimes we feel as though we can't resist our sinful impulses. But a Christian will not continue to deliberately sin. With the help of the Holy Spirit, we have the capacity to please God because we have the ability to choose to do those things God wants us to do.

Children of God (8:14-17)

Those who are led by the Spirit—that is, those who are true believers—are children of God. In Romans 6:22,

Paul said that those who are set free from the slavery of sin become slaves of God. Here he tells us what that really means. Those who choose to become slaves to God and righteousness receive the Holy Spirit, who not only gives life but also makes us children of God. This is a huge benefit! We don't have to act like slaves because we have been adopted into God's family.

In the Roman world, adoption was common. Douglas Moo writes: "It was a legal institution by which a person could adopt a child and confer on that child all the legal rights and privileges that would accrue to a natural child." Here's the deal. We were born as children of Adam, and his inheritance was death. But now we have been adopted by God, and His inheritance is life. What does this mean for us? It means that right now we have personal and direct access to God. We can go to Him as a child goes to a loving father, and we can call Him "Daddy" (that's the meaning of "Father" or "Abba" in verse 15).

Our adoption also means that we have an inheritance. The treasures and riches of our heavenly Father are ours. In addition, we are co-heirs with Christ of all that God has planned for the future. These blessings will come when Jesus returns in glory and takes us to heaven (John 14:1-4). However, Paul includes a qualifier: As co-heirs with Christ, sharing in His glory, we also have to share in His suffering.

Suffering Now, Glory Later (8:18-30)

As bad as they seem, our troubles on this earth are small and temporary, whereas the glory that is waiting for us—the glory we will share with Christ—is great and eternal.

Creation Is Groaning (8:18-22)

Have you ever heard someone refer to a natural disaster as an "act of God"? The phrase seems to imply that God causes floods, earthquakes, and hurricanes, and we can do nothing about it. The truth is that God doesn't have to cause such acts. When Adam and Eve sinned, they weren't alone in receiving God's punishment. The earth itself was cursed (Genesis 3:17-18), and now all creation is waiting for that curse to be lifted. In the meantime, the effects of sin add to the physical plight of humanity on this planet. Just as the glory of God can be seen in God's creation (Psalm 19:1-6), the sin of the human race can also be seen in our world.

We Are Groaning (8:23-25)

Creation is groaning, and so are we, even though we have the Holy Spirit to remind us of our future glory. Have you ever experienced the pressures of financial loss? Then you know what Paul is talking about. Do you know someone whose body is being ravaged by cancer? Are you in pain? Are you fighting a life-threatening illness? Then you know what groaning is like.

Does your heart ache for those in our world who are starving? Do you hurt for those trapped beneath the fist of a ruthless tyrant? In your groaning, you can rest in the hope you have in Christ. Someday you will receive your spiritual inheritance, including a new body. Someday the ills of our world will be healed.

The Holy Spirit Helps Us (8:26-27)

Creation groans and we groan, but we are not alone. The Holy Spirit groans too—for us! When we hurt so bad that we don't even know what to pray for or how to pray, the Holy Spirit helps us in our distress by literally praying and pleading to God for us. And God, who knows our hearts and knows what the Spirit is saying, hears our prayers. He understands what we are going through, thanks to the work of the Holy Spirit in our life.

God Has Called Us (8:28-30)

Now we come to one of the most comforting and often-quoted verses in the Bible. But it's often misinterpreted to mean that God uses everything that happens to us to bring us "good things." According to James Boice, here's what Paul had in mind:

- The "good" refers to "become like his Son" in 8:29. This doesn't mean that good things will happen to us, but that God will use the things in our life to conform us more to the image of Jesus.

- Not everything in our life *is* good, but God can and will use everything *for* our good.

The Best Call of All

Romans 8:29-30 contains five Lofty Theological Words and concepts, sometimes referred to as the "order of salvation." Let's walk through these one at a time:

1. **God *knew* us in advance.** This doesn't mean that God knew in advance who would receive Him by faith and then chose them to be saved. Rather, as the *Life Application Commentary* says, "God's foreknowledge refers to his intimate knowledge of us and our relationship with him based on his choosing us."

2. **God *chose* us to become like His Son.** This means He chose—or elected—us for a single purpose: to be like Jesus.

3. **God *called* us to come to Him.** God calls every person He knows and chooses. This is a divine, internal call to salvation.

4. **God gave us a *right standing* with Himself.** When God's chosen ones respond to His call by faith, He justifies them.

5. **God promised us His *glory*.** Finally, when the time comes, God will glorify those He has known, chosen, called, and justified.

If God Is for Us (8:31-39)

"What can we say about such wonderful things as these?" So begins one of the most glorious and encouraging passages in all of Scripture. Everything Paul has talked about—our calling by God in the past, our life in the Spirit now, and our future in Christ—adds up to a remarkable conclusion: "If God is for us, who can ever be against us?" Paul is saying, "With God on your side, you will never lose!"

Our position as believers is completely secure. Nothing in heaven or on earth can alter God's plan to glorify those He has known, chosen, called, and justified. And to show us just how secure we are, Paul considers several scenarios.

No One Can Ever Be Against Us (8:31-32)

Spiritually, we are invincible. How do we know? What evidence do we have that God will make good on His word? We have the historical reality of Jesus Christ, sent by God to die for us so we don't have to die, and raised to life by God so we can live. We can trust that

God, who gave us Christ, will give us everything else He has promised.

No One Dares Accuse Us (8:33)

This isn't just any accusation (such as someone accusing you of being intolerant in your beliefs). This refers to our chief accuser, Satan (Zechariah 3:1; Revelation 12:10). God will disregard any accusations leveled against those He has "chosen for his own" because He has already justified us in Christ.

No One Will Condemn Us (8:34)

We are no longer under condemnation. This applies now and in the future. In the divine court of heaven, our verdict is set because of Christ: *not guilty.* Even now, as Satan attempts to bring new (and sometimes true) charges against us, Jesus is at the right hand of God, praying and pleading for us.

Nothing Can Separate Us—Part 1 (8:35-36)

As if we need more evidence that God's chosen ones are secure, Paul lists seven real dangers in this world and tells us that none of these can separate us from Christ's love. He is not saying that these things won't happen—in fact, Christians have always had to endure such afflictions—but these can never nullify our relationship with Christ.

- *trouble*—difficult circumstances
- *calamity*—deep distress or tragedy
- *persecution*—for our beliefs
- *hunger*—lack of physical nourishment
- *cold*—lack of shelter or clothing

- *danger*—any kind of threat
- *death*—for the sake of Christ

Nothing Can Separate Us—Part 2 (8:37-39)

Here Paul lets it all loose. In a sweeping conclusion to this awesome chapter, he throws in everything that people might think could possibly interrupt or harm our relationship with our loving Lord, and he concludes that absolutely nothing can do it. As a result, we won't just slide into heaven by the skin of our teeth. "Overwhelming victory is ours through Christ, who loved us" (8:37). We are safe from assaults—not only in the natural world but also in the supernatural world. Even death, the last and greatest enemy, can't separate us from God's love. Truly the love of God that is revealed in Christ Jesus is the strongest, most trustworthy thing of all.

■ ▨ ▧

$\mathcal{S}$tudy the $\mathcal{W}$ord

1. You are no longer under condemnation. What does that mean to you on a spiritual level? What does it mean on a practical level?

2. Review Paul's description of people who are dominated by their sinful nature. Are people in this condition saved? Why or why not?

3. How can you cooperate with the work of the Holy
   Spirit in your life? How can you hinder His work?

4. Think about your adoption by God and your inheritance with Christ. What are some treasures (8:17)
   you will share in heaven? What are some treasures
   you share now? What difference should these treasures make in your life?

5. In what ways does sinful humanity add to the groaning of our planet?

6. What is your response to Romans 8:29-30? Does the "order of salvation" make sense to you, or are you wrestling with what it means?

7. Review the list of seven real world dangers in Romans 8:35-36. Why have Christians through the ages had to endure these things? Why hasn't God protected us from them?

An Important Parenthesis

Congratulations! You have made it through the first and longest section of Romans. You've wrestled with such LTWs as *imputation, justification, sanctification,* and *glorification.* You have debated—and will continue to debate—what being chosen and called by God means. Now we come to Romans 9–11, three Bible chapters we're going to cover in just one chapter of this study. That's because this section of Romans is like a parenthesis between the first eight chapters, where Paul tells us what to *believe* (this is the *doctrinal* section), and the last five chapters, where Paul advises us how to *behave* (this is the *practical* section).

So where does that leave this middle section? Here Paul has one main concern: Israel. More to the point, Paul wants us to know that God has always had a purpose and a plan for His chosen people, and He fully intends to keep the promises He has made to them. In these three chapters, Paul is going to deal with three important topics that are universal in their importance and implication: God's *election,* our *responsibility,* and God's *sovereignty.* So even though the topic of Romans 9–11 is Israel, the focus is on God and our responsibility before Him.

Chapter 9

God and Israel

Romans 9–11

What's Ahead

- [ ] God Chose Israel (Romans 9)

- [ ] Israel Did Not Choose Christ (Romans 10)

- [ ] God's Plans for Israel Have Not Changed (Romans 11)

*W*hen is the last time your heart broke for someone who is not a Christian? Has your heart *ever* been broken for someone who is separated from God, walking down a path leading to death rather than life? Wouldn't you agree that as Christians, many of us are much too easygoing about the condition of the lost and their eternal destiny apart from God? We need to seek God's forgiveness and ask Him to give us compassionate hearts as we consider how to relate to people who don't know the God who saved us.

God doesn't expect you to bear the weight of the world on your shoulders, but He has called you to reach out to the people He has put in your path whether they are family members, friends, neighbors, coworkers, or strangers. Of course, God doesn't expect you to go it alone. He wants you to trust Him. As you study this section of Romans, watch how Paul blends his concern for the lost with His trust in the sovereignty and mercy of God.

God Chose Israel (Romans 9)

Paul starts this chapter by identifying himself with the people of Israel (he will do the same at the beginning of Romans 10 and 11). He feels sorrow for them, and yet he is baffled that people with so much spiritual privilege could be so blind to the truth.

Paul's Heart Breaks for Israel (9:1-5)

Notice the emotion behind Paul's words in these opening verses of Romans 9. Because his Jewish brothers and sisters aren't saved, he is in anguish. At the same time, he wrestles with some obvious facts concerning Israel. They have everything going for them, yet they have rejected the Messiah their own prophets foretold. Paul's internal dialogue over this matter prompts four questions. The issues raised by these questions go to the foundation of the Christian experience because they don't just concern Israel. Ultimately, the answers reveal the heart of God and His love for each of us.

Question #1: Has God Failed to Fulfill His Promise? (9:6-13)

Paul knew then, as we know now, that God made a remarkable promise to Israel—that He would make them a great nation, bless them, and then bless all the families of the earth through them. He gave this blessing to Abraham (Genesis 12:1-3), and He reaffirmed it to Jacob (Genesis 35:9-13). Has this promise failed because the Jews rejected their Messiah, whom God sent to bless them and the world? Not at all. The failure was with Israel, not with God or His promise. Israel had the opportunity to respond to the Good News message of Jesus but failed to do so.

$\mathcal{T}$wo $\mathcal{I}$sraels

John Stott points out that in fact God's promise has never been in danger of failing. Here's why. Israel has always had two kinds of descendents: the *physical* descendents of Israel and the *spiritual* descendents. Even though many physical descendents have rejected God's promise, many spiritual descendents (Paul is an example) have responded to the Good News message of Jesus and received God's promised blessing. This is what Paul means when he says, "not everyone born into a Jewish family is truly a Jew!" (9:6).

Paul gives two illustrations of prominent Jews to show the difference between the physical and spiritual nation of Israel. In both cases, Paul says that God chose one person over another: He chose Isaac over Ishmael (9:7) and Jacob over Esau (9:13). In fact, God chose Jacob over Esau even before they were born, "according to his own plan" (9:11).

Question #2: Was God Being Unfair? (9:14-18)

Paul asks the question you are probably asking: Is God being unfair by choosing one person over another? And more to the issue of Israel and the rest of us, is God being fair by choosing—the LTW here is *electing*—some to be saved, leaving others to die in their sins?

This is a really big, tough issue that troubles more people than perhaps anything else in the Bible. We're not going to pretend that we can solve this for you in a few sentences, but we do want to stimulate your thinking. Talk about this business of election in your group or discuss it with other mature believers. Try not to get overly defensive or take a strong offensive position, and avoid putting human characteristics on God. Remember that He's God and you're not. (Before you go any further, read Isaiah 55:8-9.)

This matter of election involves two things:

1. God's Sovereignty

Basically, this means God can do whatever He chooses. God is the only self-existent Being, who created everything and keeps everything together. He can do anything with His creation that He chooses. However, God cannot act in a malicious or unfair manner towards His creation because by His very nature He is—among other things—loving, holy, righteous, and just. We may not understand everything God does—in fact, we're guaranteed not to—but we can trust Him that everything He does is right and true.

2. God's Mercy

Paul addresses this in 9:14-16. The fact that God has mercy on anyone at all is amazing. Think back to the human condition Paul described earlier in Romans. We have been rebelling against God and rejecting Him since He first created us. None of us seek God on our own, and none of us deserve God. Yet God offers salvation out of His merciful love because, as John Stott says, "the basis

on which God deals with sinners is not justice but
mercy." If God dealt with us according to His justice,
none of us would be saved. "The point," writes R.C.
Sproul, "is not in God's overlooking of some, but in His
mercy toward *anyone at all.*"

Question #3: Why Does God Blame People for Not Listening? (9:19-29)

Another way to phrase this question is this: How can
God hold people accountable for the choices He makes?
Paul's answer goes back to God's sovereignty and mercy.
As the potter, God has the right to shape the clay into
anything He wants. He has the right to exercise His judgment, and He has the right to show His mercy. Although
we may ask questions of God, we have no right to question God. We must accept that His actions are always
compatible with His nature.

Question #4: What Shall We Say About These Things? (9:30-33)

First of all, rather than criticizing God for allowing
some Jews to fail, we should be praising Him for justi-
fying some Gentiles, especially since they weren't even
seeking Him. Truth is, in Paul's day the Good News
message was being preached to Jews and Gentiles alike,
and the Gentiles were more responsive. Most of the
Jews could not get past their dependence on the law. In
this way Jesus became a stone that caused them to
stumble because He showed them that their works
didn't make them right with God. Of course, Jesus is a
stumbling block to anyone who thinks they are good
enough to satisfy God. But those who believe in Jesus

and receive what He has done for them will not be disappointed.

Israel Did Not Choose Christ (Romans 10)

Whereas Romans 9 deals with *God's election*, the emphasis in Romans 10 shifts to *our responsibility*. In Romans 9, we looked at what God has done in the past. In this chapter we will look at what we need to do now. Again, the topic is Israel, but the application is universal.

Clinging to Their Own Way (10:1-4)

Once again Paul's heart breaks for the Jewish people. He longs for them to be saved. They are without a doubt zealous for God, but zeal and good intentions alone can't save them. The same is true for us today. People who stubbornly refuse to accept God's plan in favor of "clinging to their own way of getting right with God" (verse 3) are never going to please God. God's way is so simple, yet people refuse to go along with it—to their own peril.

The Way to Be Saved (10:5-13)

We don't need to bring Christ down from heaven—He has already come! We don't need to fish Him out of the grave—He is risen! Jesus has done everything necessary to secure our right standing before God. We don't have to follow legalistic rituals to please God. We don't have to go to a mountain in Tibet to find God. He is right here in front of us in the person of Jesus. Because He is as close as our mouths and our hearts, the way to be saved is both simple and profound.

- *"Confess with your mouth that Jesus is Lord."* John Stott says this is the "earliest and simplest of all Christian creeds." This is the outward verbal expression of an inward belief. In fact, you can't separate confession from belief. A confession without belief is meaningless.

- **"Believe in your heart that God raised him from the dead."** This is not just believing *in* God (even the demons have this kind of belief—James 2:19). This is believing that the risen Lord Jesus Christ is the only way to be justified before God.

> This is not salvation by slogan but by faith, that is, by an intelligent faith which lays hold of the positive message of "the righteousness that is by faith."
>
> —John Stott

The Need to Evangelize (10:14-15)

Here are two verses for anyone who thinks God's election negates the need for evangelism. Scripture is very clear that those of us who have been called by God need to tell others about Him. Paul presents a chain of events leading up to the point where someone believes in God and then calls on Him.

- *Calling* on the Lord is based on *believing*.

- *Believing* the Lord is dependent on *hearing*.

- *Hearing* results from someone *telling*.

- *Telling* comes from *sending*.

- *Sending* comes from *Jesus* (see Mark 16:15).

You Were Called and You Are Being Called

If you are a Christian, God called you to salvation. But your calling doesn't end there. God is calling you now to share His Good News message with people He puts in your path. Stop right now and think of at least three people you need to tell about Jesus. Then pray and ask God to give you opportunities to share Jesus with them.

Refusing to Obey (10:16-21)

Why has Israel continued to reject God's plan for their salvation? Many Gentiles have accepted it, so why not many Jews? Have they not been given enough chances to hear? Has the message not been clear enough? Have they not understood? As a nation, the Jews have considered themselves to be God's *only* chosen people, but they have missed the last part of God's promise to them—that *all* the families of the earth would be blessed through them. God has been patient with Israel and gracious to them despite their disobedience. Meanwhile, His salvation is available to all people, Jews and Gentiles alike.

God's Plans for Israel Have Not Changed (Romans 11)

For the third time in three chapters, Paul reminds us that he is a Jew, descended from Abraham. From his perspective as a child of God and one who is being guided by the Holy Spirit, God's plans for Israel are still in place.

God Has Not Rejected Israel (11:1-10)

The very fact that Paul—a Jew who once persecuted Christians—has been saved is evidence that "God has not rejected his own people, whom he chose from the very beginning" (11:2). Paul then offers Elijah, the great prophet of Israel, as proof. At one time Elijah thought he was the only believing person left in Israel (1 Kings 19:10). But he was wrong. There was a remnant of 7000. "It's the same today," says Paul, "for not all the Jews have turned away from God" (11:5).

However, the hard reality is this: "Most of the Jews have not found the favor of God they are looking for so earnestly" (11:7). God has chosen some, but the rest are in a kind of "deep sleep" (11:8). Why is this? Is God being cruel or unfair? Again, we must appeal to God's sovereignty and His character, so God can't help but be loving and fair. The more reasonable explanation is that Israel's continual disobedience and argumentative spirit (10:21) have dulled their senses to God. From our perspective it may seem as though God has hardened their hearts, but from His perspective, God has simply allowed them to follow their rebellious inclinations. God has not rejected Israel; Israel has rejected God.

Israel Will Recover (11:11-24)

Have God's people "stumbled beyond recovery?" For the tenth time in Romans, Paul answers his own question with, "Of course not!" So what is God doing? In His sovereign mercy and grace, God has used Israel's rejection of Christ in order to bring salvation to the Gentiles. And that's just the first link in God's salvation chain. As the Gentiles embrace the Messiah, the Jews will become more and more envious and will want this salvation for themselves (11:11). This in turn will lead to a greater blessing for the whole world "when the Jews finally accept it" (11:12).

Something to Ponder

If you have come to the conclusion that Israel's rejection wasn't an accident, you are correct in your thinking. As the *Life Application Bible Commentary* puts it, "Israel's rejection of Christ was part of God's plan all along." And that plan, of course, was to send the Good News message of Jesus throughout the world, which would not have happened (theoretically speaking) if the Jews had not rejected Christ.

Paul uses an allegory of an olive tree to illustrate how God has been working with Jews and Gentiles and their belief (11:17-24). This illustration includes a warning to believing Gentiles—don't get smug (11:19-21)—as well as an encouraging message about unbelieving Jews— they still have hope (11:23-24).

Still His Chosen People (11:25-32)

As Paul begins to wrap up this chapter, he admits something we're all thinking. This is all a pretty big mystery. But it's not a mystery without purpose. To summarize:

- Many Jews have refused to believe in Jesus.

- Their unbelief opened up the blessings of God to the Gentiles.

- The Jews are still God's chosen people because God never goes back on a promise.

- Just as the Gentiles were once rebellious to God, the Jews are now rebellious.

- Someday the Jews will share in God's mercy, which the Gentiles now enjoy.

Who Can Know What God Is Thinking? (11:33-36)

Isn't Paul's response here interesting? Rather than saying, "This stuff is just a little too much for me," he expresses his joy by saying, "What a wonderful God we have!" Read these last four verses in Romans 11 as if you were singing a hymn of praise to God. Don't be like those who criticize God because they don't agree with Him, or ignore Him because they don't understand His ways. We need to praise God for His power and thank Him for His mercy.

■ ■ ■

$\mathcal{S}$tudy the $\mathcal{W}$ord

1. When was the last time your heart broke for someone who is lost without Christ? What did you do?

2. Read Romans 9:4-5. List the seven special privileges that God gave to Israel.

3. Before reading this chapter, had you ever thought about the concept of God's election? How are you dealing with the idea that God chooses *some* people—rather than *all* people—to be saved?

4. In Romans 9:18 Paul writes that God "chooses to make some people refuse to listen." This describes the process of God's "hardening" the hearts of some people. How does a heart become hardened? Does God do it, or is the individual ultimately responsible? Read Hebrews 3:7-8.

5. What would happen if God's sovereignty did not work together with His mercy?

6. Think about the two different "calls" God has made on your life: the call to salvation and the call to share His Good News message with others. Describe how you have responded to each call.

7. What would you say to a person who says, "I'm just doing what's right in my own eyes"?

8. Why do you think God has been so patient with Israel? Do you think God still has a relationship with the physical descendants of Israel? What special privileges are waiting for those Jews who do respond to the Good News message?

Build on Your Foundation

Every building project begins with the foundation. You can't just put up walls and a roof on a pile of dirt and expect it to stand. Without a sure foundation, everything else you build crumbles. At the same time, a foundation is laid so something can be built upon it. Without a structure on top of it, a foundation doesn't serve its true purpose.

The Christian life has only one sure foundation, and that's Jesus Christ (1 Corinthians 3:11). If you build your life on anything else, it will crumble. But Jesus didn't give His life for you just so you could sit back and wait for the glory train. God saved you so you could build on the foundation of His Son by doing those good things He planned for you long ago (Ephesians 2:10). Or to put it in the language of our little metaphor, Jesus laid a foundation so you could build something on it.

So far in Romans, Paul has informed us about our foundation. From this chapter until the end of his letter, he's going to tell us how to build upon it. Now that we know who we are in Jesus, we're going to learn how we're supposed to live as Christians.

Chapter 10

How to Live as a Christian

Romans 12

What's Ahead

- ☐ Change the Way You Think (12:1-2)
- ☐ Use Your Gifts (12:3-8)
- ☐ Really Love Others (12:9-13)
- ☐ Live in Peace (12:14-21)

An old saying says, "Practice what you preach." That's what Romans 12 and the next four chapters are all about. But in this case, God wants us to practice what Paul has been preaching. He wants us to apply what we've been learning. God doesn't just want us to know all the good things He has done for us. God wants us to do good things! He wants us to build a beautiful structure on top of the foundation of Jesus Christ. And just how do you do that? You're about to find out.

Change the Way You Think (12:1-2)

You get a pretty good clue that what Paul is about to say is very important to him—and to us—from Paul's language. He is pleading, urging, literally begging us to put into action the things we have been learning. In the first two verses of this chapter, Paul outlines three action steps toward living a Christian life that is pleasing to God and productive for us.

Be Intelligent and Intentional (12:1)

The first thing Paul asks is that we give our bodies to God as living and holy sacrifices. This implies that not just any kind of casual sacrifice will do. We are to fully commit our bodies in every dimension—physical, intellectual, emotional, and spiritual. Because our bodies are given to us by God so we can live in this world, we are to subject all that we are to God and His will for our lives.

Doing this is a sacred act, translated by the NIV as a "spiritual act of worship." We like the old KJV translation: "reasonable service." This implies two things. First, committing ourselves to God and His will should be reasonable, rational, and thoughtful. Mindless devotion has no place in the Christian life. God expects us to use our intellectual abilities as we serve Him. Second, we need to realize that we are in service to God. In the business world, good service doesn't happen by accident. It takes careful, thoughtful planning. Why should we do any less as we serve God? He gave us life through His Son. We must give our lives intelligently and intentionally for Him.

Refuse to Be Conformed (12:2a)

Whereas 12:1 talks about making a definite commitment to give God our reasonable service, 12:2 tells us how to keep that commitment. This has two parts. Paul phrases the first part in the negative—he urges us to *not* conform to the culture. The NLT says, "Don't copy the behavior and customs of this world." The NIV translates this as "Do not conform any longer to the pattern of this world." Both renderings convey the idea that we are to avoid being absorbed by the culture to the point that others can't tell us apart from those who are still controlled by their sin natures.

The Value of Different Translations

There is tremendous value in using different translations as you study the Bible. We are using the *New Living Translation* as our main text, but we gain additional insights by using a variety of other Bible translations. You can do the same thing. Settle on one Bible translation for your everyday reading, but incorporate one or two other Bible versions into your systematic study.

Refusing to conform to the customs of the world begins with resisting the philosophies and attitudes of a culture whose values stand in opposition to God. Apart from God and His eternal perspective, people operate on the principle that this life is all they have. Humanism and hedonism are the dominant worldviews. God has a different view and so should we. Our worldview needs to be anchored to eternity.

Let God Transform You (12:2b)

Refusing to be conformed to the culture also has a positive aspect to it. Since we still have to live among sin-controlled people, God wants us to live in the world as salt and light so that our "good deeds shine out for all to see" (Matthew 5:16). We have two reasons for doing this. First, the world needs the influence of Christians.

As bad as you think things are now, imagine how much darker and more hostile the culture would be without the influence of people controlled by the Holy Spirit. Second, God uses His children as witnesses to the Good News of Jesus Christ so that others will come out of the kingdom of darkness and into the kingdom of light (refer back to Romans 10:14-15).

The way we maintain a positive witness in a negative world is by letting God transform us—that is, change us for the better—by changing the way we think. The NIV phrases this, "by the renewing of your mind." The mind is a powerful force in our lives. The book of Proverbs says, "For as he thinks within himself, so he is" (Proverbs 23:7 NASB). Unless our minds are wrapped around God on a daily basis, we won't be transformed, and the culture will dominate our bodies.

On a practical level, how do you let God transform your thinking? Here are three things you can do every day.

1. *Let the Holy Spirit do His work.* God has given each believer the Holy Spirit to teach us and to remind us of Jesus (John 14:26). Through our hearts and our minds, the Holy Spirit's job is to guide us into all truth (John 16:13). Letting God change our thinking begins with letting the Holy Spirit control our lives.

2. *Study God's Word.* Unless we are engaged in daily, deliberate Bible study, God will not be able to transform the way we think. It's as simple as that. We need to get it in our heads and our hearts that God's Word is God's personal message to us,

telling us how to live in a way that pleases Him (2 Timothy 3:16).

3. **Understand the culture.** Though we are not to conform to the culture, we are to be *in* the culture and understand what makes it tick. We should strive to be intelligent, informed, loving people who will relate to others in a way that will invite them to ask us about the hope that is within us (1 Peter 3:15).

Use Your Gifts (12:3-8)

Paul now shifts from how we should live in the *culture* to how we should live in the *church*. By "church" he is referring to the universal church, defined by Wayne Grudem as "the community of all true believers for all time."

Live in the Body (12:3-5)

Jesus Christ is the head of the church, which is characterized as a body (Ephesians 5:23). Paul builds on this body image to show us that just as a physical body needs all of its parts to function effectively, the spiritual body needs each of us. Here are three principles to keep in mind as you think of yourself as a member of the universal church as well as a member of a local church:

- **We are all one body.** Just like a big toe can't live apart from the foot, and the foot can't live apart from the body, we can't live and function apart from the body of Christ. This speaks to the *unity* of the body.

- **Each of us has a different work to do.** Your body wouldn't be much good if all your body parts tried to perform the same function (we'll let your imagination run with that image). Similarly, the church needs the *diversity* of its members in order to do the job God has called it to do.

- **Each of us needs all the others.** We can never say that our role in the church is more important than someone else's. Body life is one of *mutuality,* in which each member depends on the gifts of the others.

Discover Your Spiritual Gift and Use It (12:6-8)

God has given each of us "the ability to do certain things well" (12:6). This is referring to spiritual gifts, not natural abilities. Although your spiritual gift may be useful in your work outside the church, it is properly defined by Grudem as "any ability that is empowered by the Holy Spirit and used in any ministry of the church." Paul goes on to list seven gifts—prophecy, serving, teaching, encouraging, sharing money with others, leadership, and showing kindness or mercy—but this is not an exhaustive list. In his letters to the Corinthians and the Ephesians, Paul includes more lists (1 Corinthians 7:7; 12:8-10,28; Ephesians 4:11). When you look at all of these spiritual gifts, you can see that the church has no shortage of abilities. What's often lacking is our willingness to discover our gifts and use them.

Really Love Others (12:9-13)

Merely accepting and respecting the gifts of others is not enough. God didn't create us anew in Christ Jesus just so we could coexist like a well-oiled machine. God wants us to *really love* one another.

What Kind of Love? (12:9)

Our love for each other must be sincere and from the heart. The Greek work for *love* here is *agape,* which is the same as God's love for us. In our love we are to adopt God's attitude by rejecting evil and standing up for good.

What Love Looks Like (12:10-13)

The Greek word for love in 12:10 is *philadelphia,* or "brotherly love." This is love in action. Here's how we love others in this way:

- Honor each other by showing appreciation for them and their gifts.

- Serve the Lord, and in doing so serve others.

- When someone in the body is in trouble, we need to pray.

- When someone in the body is in need, we need to help out.

Live in Peace (12:14-21)

After telling us how to live in harmony with our fellow believers, Paul now shifts his attention to the ways we can live in peace with our enemies.

How to Handle Persecution (12:14)

Paul's advice for handling persecution must have been a bit of a shock to the Roman believers, especially since the persecution Paul is referring to is the real deal. This isn't the kind of passive persecution we may face from time to time. This is active persecution at the hands of a hostile world. Even though we may not know what such persecution may feel like, we can be sure that the Roman Christians knew, as do many of our world today. Everett Harrison writes:

> Persecution in some form or another was so common in the experience of the early church that Paul is able to assume as a matter of course that it is a factor in the lives of his readers. If such treatment is not encountered in our society, we can at least cultivate the readiness to meet it and so fulfill the injunction in spirit.

So how do we pray for those who persecute Christians? It involves two things:

- praying for their forgiveness

- praying for a change of heart

This is definitely not the natural response of persecuted people, but it is the result of persecuted people transformed by Christ.

How to Make Friends with an Enemy (12:15-17)

The culture says to love your friends and hate your enemies, but Paul says we are to make friends with our enemies. He gives us four ways to do this:

- *Share their joy and divide their sorrow.* This is the basis of empathy, which is a rare commodity in today's culture. People will criticize, people will even sympathize, but they will rarely empathize, making empathy a wonderful way to turn an enemy into a friend.

- *Live in harmony with everyone.* Be easygoing, not contentious. Sometimes people make enemies out of their neighbors by being picky. Remember, Jesus said we are to love—not loathe—our neighbor.

- *Be a regular Joe (or Jane).* Nobody likes a showoff or a boaster. Just be a humble person who enjoys hanging out with ordinary people.

- *Don't try to get even.* We are often tempted to strike back—verbally or otherwise—at someone who strikes out at us. Let it go. Show your love and keep your honor.

How to Face a Hostile World (12:18-21)

Whether you are experiencing conflict at home, at the office, or in your neighborhood, refuse to be the instigator of trouble and instead be the maker of peace (Matthew 5:9). And whatever you do, don't take revenge. God is the only one who has the right to take revenge, because only He acts in a righteous manner all the time. Instead of repaying evil with evil, we need to conquer evil with good. Think about this: Someone who has deliberately wronged you will expect you to get back at them. If you choose to love that person in return, how do you think that will make them feel? Everett Harrison says it best: "To receive kindness, to see love when it seems uncalled for, can melt the hardest heart."

■ ■ ■

$\mathcal{S}$tudy the $\mathcal{W}$ord

1. In what ways does your mind influence the person you are and the things you do? How does your mind influence your relationships?

2. What's the best kind of worship? How can you do this when you are in church? How about the rest of the week? What happens when we worship God in spirit, but not in truth? (See John 4:24.)

3. In what ways might we easily become conformed to the way the culture thinks? How does thinking like the culture cause you to behave like the culture? What are you doing now to allow God to transform your thinking?

   What if you change your thinking, and that changes your behavior, and you end up standing out in school, at your work, or in your family? How will you handle the criticism?

4. Review the lists of spiritual gifts in Romans, 1 Corinthians, and Ephesians. What is one of your spiritual gifts? How are you using it in the body of Christ? If you can't identify a spiritual gift, how can you discover it? What might happen to those who never bother to discover and use their spiritual gifts?

5. How would you respond to a Christian who doesn't think going to church is necessary? What Scripture would you use in your response?

6. Compare Paul's teaching on persecution in Romans 12:14 with the teaching of Jesus in Matthew 5:43-45. How does this teaching help Christians deal with persecution? How does it help those who persecute Christians?

7. When was the last time you tried to make friends with an enemy? What did you do, and what happened?

Getting Along with the Government

Getting along with other Christians (who are supposed to love you) or even unbelievers (who sometimes oppose you) is one thing, but how do you get along with your government (who loves to tax you), especially when you feel restricted or oppressed?

Undoubtedly this was a big issue for the first-century Roman Christians, who lived in the grip of one of history's most powerful states. That's why Paul has decided to include this hot topic in his field manual for Christians. Not only do we need to relate in a Christlike manner to people—believers and unbelievers alike—but we also need to relate in a Christlike manner to the government in authority over us.

Paul then reminds us that we need to live with urgency. This is no time to sleep on the job in darkness. We need to be wide awake in the light.

Chapter 11

Living as a Citizen of This World

Romans 13

What's Ahead

- [ ] The Christian and Authority (13:1-7)

- [ ] The Christian and Culture (13:8-14)

*A*s a Christian you have a dual citizenship: You were born as a citizen of God's natural world, and you were reborn as a citizen of God's supernatural world. Your job as a Christian is to live responsibly in both worlds. Paul has been dealing with the ways we can live as effective spiritual citizens, and now he turns his attention to the ways we can live as effective world citizens.

Paul probably had several reasons for addressing this topic. Remember, one of his purposes for writing this letter to the Roman Christians was to prepare them to take the Good News message of Jesus to the farthest corners of the Roman Empire. He knew they could best do that as cooperative citizens rather than renegades. Paul also wanted to instruct his readers on the nature and God-given authority of government.

The Christian and Authority (13:1-7)

Every activity, individual, and institution on earth is subject to the sovereignty of God. Just as an earthquake does not happen unless God allows it, no government has been established apart from God's sovereign power. Paul states this even stronger. "All governments have been placed in power by God." Does that mean evil dictators are in power because God put them there? We'll cover that sticky issue a little later, but first we need to look at why God wants us to obey the government, also known as the state.

> A state is essentially a body of men who have banded themselves together, who have covenanted together, to maintain certain relationships between each other by the observance of certain laws.
>
> —*William Barclay*

Obey the Government (13:1-5)

Biblical commentator William Barclay suggests three reasons why Christians are called to obey the government.

1. Governments provide services.

As spiritual citizens, we enjoy certain benefits because we are each a part of Christ's body. As citizens of a nation, we enjoy certain benefits because we are each a part of a national body. Most of these benefits, such as municipal services and law enforcement, would not be ours if we didn't band together to form governments. We have these services because God has established governments and asked us to obey them. Because we have these benefits, we also have a duty to support the government that provides them. Barclay writes: "A man has a duty to the state, and must discharge that duty even if Nero is on the throne."

2. Governments provide protection.

One of the primary functions of a state is to protect its citizens by creating and enforcing laws. Without the rule of law, the bad guys would make life miserable for the rest of us law-abiding citizens, and civilized society as we know it would not exist.

3. Governments keep the world from chaos.

In Paul's day the Roman government was the world's peacekeeper. Even though Christians were restricted in some ways, in other ways they had enormous freedom. Barclay points out that the *pax Romana* (peace of Rome) enabled Christian missionaries such as Paul to take the Good News throughout the Roman Empire without worrying about borders.

Pay Your Taxes (13:6-7)

Now here's a sensitive subject. We may pay our taxes, but we often do it grudgingly. That's not the spirit in which Paul says we should support those who govern us. We need to pay our taxes with respect and honor. The overarching principle here is that the government needs money to provide services and protection for its citizens and to keep peace in the world. The more specific principle is that the government can't do what God has ordained it to do without workers. Not accidentally, we call those who work for the state "public servants," and in some cultures high-ranking government officials are called "ministers." In a way, government workers are serving God as ministers by carrying out His mandate to govern. We need to support, honor, and respect those who minister to us, whether in the church or in the world.

*M*ust *W*e *A*lways *O*bey the *G*overnment?

Is disobeying the government ever right? Even those of us who live in a republic that offers unprecedented and unparalleled freedom, services, and protection sometimes wonder if we have a right—and maybe even a responsibility—to disobey our government. And what about Christians living under regimes that forbid them to openly practice their faith in Jesus Christ? What are they supposed to do? Here are some guidelines from Douglas Moo:

> Paul could hardly be naive about the potential for governments to be unjust...Probably, then, what Paul is doing in Romans 13:1-4 is describing how governments are *supposed to function.* Perhaps he also implies that the submission of Christians to rulers need not take the form of obedience when governments do not implement divine justice.

Here is a good way to look at it. We need to obey the government, but when our obedience to the government comes into conflict with our obedience to Christ, then we must defer to Christ. R.C. Sproul writes:

> As long as the state does not prevent us from fulfilling this greater responsibility, there is no problem. But if by its ordinances or policies a government begins to limit believers' ability to do what God clearly requires of them, Christians have no choice—they must disobey the state.

At the same time, we need to trust God that He will deal with wicked government rulers and regimes in His own way and in His own time. Whenever a ruthless dictator is toppled, thank God that He is sovereign over all governments.

The Christian and Culture (13:8-14)

We should always pay our debts, whether to the government in the form of taxes or to a lender. One kind of debt, however, we should never stop paying on. This debt is the one that should guide how a Christian should live in the culture.

The Debt of Love (13:8-10)

Here is the only debt we should continue to pay as long as we live—for two reasons:

- God loved us enough to send His Son, so we need to love each other (1 John 4:11).

- Christ commanded us to love our neighbor as ourselves (Matthew 22:39).

In fact, by keeping the commandment to love our neighbor, we fulfill all the other commandments. Paul tells us how this works by pulling four examples from the Ten Commandments:

- *Adultery*—Those who continually pay on the debt of love will respect others and act in an honorable manner at all times.

- *Murder*—Those who continually pay on the debt of love seek to build up, not destroy.

- *Stealing*—Those who continually pay on the debt of love are more concerned with giving than getting.

- *Coveting*—Those who continually pay on the debt of love are more concerned with helping others than possessing what others have.

Redeem the Time (13:11-14)

This next section is interesting. At first glance Paul appears to suggest that Jesus is going to return any time, so we need to be ready because the time is short. In fact, the first-century Christians were eagerly awaiting Christ's return. They knew what Jesus had said: "You also must be ready all the time. For the Son of Man will come when least expected" (Matthew 24:44).

> The debt of love remains with us permanently and never leaves us.
>
> —Origen

But this isn't what Paul is saying here in 13:11. If he were, then he would have used the Greek word *chronos*—which has to do with a sequence of events—for *time* in the phrase, "time is running out." Instead he uses the word *kairos*, which refers to "meaningful time." In other words, none of us knows how much time we have left, so we need to make the time we have left as meaningful as possible.

St. Augustine and Meaningful Time

St. Augustine, one of the greatest and most influential Christian thinkers of all time, was an immoral, skeptical person who came to a point of great spiritual crisis in his life at the age of 33. In the midst of his struggle, he opened a Bible at random and turned to this exact passage of Scripture, Romans 13:11-14. The words of Paul hit him like a blinding light. He said: "How long, how long? Tomorrow, and tomorrow? Why not now? Why is there not this hour an end to my uncleanness?"

For Augustine, the realization that time was running out for him led to his conversion to Christ. You may be at that same point of realization, or you may be a Christian who has not made a decision to follow Christ fully. Either way, the time for right living is now!

We must stop living in darkness, as do those who are controlled by their sin natures, and begin living in the light, as do those who are controlled by the Holy Spirit. This process has two steps:

- *We need to take off our "dirty clothes."* Paul is asking us to get rid of our evil deeds, which he lists in detail.

- *We need to put on the armor of right living.* This involves letting the Lord Jesus Christ take control of our lives.

Rather than indulging in evil desires, we need to follow Paul's advice in his letter to the Philippians:

> *Fix your thoughts on what is true and honorable and right. Think about things that are pure and lovely and admirable. Think about things that are excellent and worthy of praise* (Philippians 4:8).

Study the Word

1. Why are some Christians so openly critical of the government? Why are Christians generally labeled as politically conservative or right-wing? Is this a fair label? Should a Christian's political views be formed by his or her faith? In what ways?

2. Compare Paul's teaching on the Christian's responsibility to the state in Romans 13 with 1 Timothy 2:1-2; Titus 3:1; and 1 Peter 2:13-17.

3. Read the story of Daniel and his relationship to the government in Daniel 1:8-21. Also read the story of Shadrach, Meshach, and Abednego in Daniel 3. Write a position statement on the Christian and civil disobedience based on these passages.

4. Read Nehemiah 2:1-8. Why might Christians want to "gain the favor of kings"? How can they do that?

5. In what practical ways can you continually pay on the debt of love to other believers? How about to non-Christians?

6. In what ways are you "redeeming the time" in your own life? What does living your life with a sense of urgency mean?

7. The Bible tells us to honor our father and mother. How can we extend this honor to other people? Give some practical ideas.

Christians Love a Good Fight

Over the centuries the church has endured some huge controversies. In the second century the church fathers defended our faith against pagan influences and philosophical heresies. In the fourth century the Council of Nicea affirmed the deity of Christ and the reality of the Trinity. In the fifth century St. Augustine clarified the doctrines of sin and grace that we take for granted today. On and on through the history of the church, false doctrines have been fought and truth has been defended by godly people who were willing to engage their minds and express their love for Jesus Christ. Because of their willingness to define and defend our faith, we can stand safely and solidly on a sure source of truth.

So what do Christians define and defend today? Are any more major doctrinal issues at stake? Perhaps, but most of the time we're defending ourselves not against doctrinal heresies but against personal attacks—from other Christians! And if we aren't on the defensive, at times we get on the offensive because we don't like the beliefs or behavior of others. The only problem is that we aren't dealing with the *essential* issues of the faith (as did our church fathers) but with peripheral or *nonessential* issues that have nothing to do with whether or not we are saved.

The first-century church was caught up in unnecessary bickering just as we are today. That's why Paul devoted a chapter and a half of Romans to helping Christians learn to live together in a community of love and grace.

Chapter 12

Living in Christian Community

Romans 14:1–15:13

What's Ahead

- Accept One Another (14:1-12)

- Don't Be a Stumbling Block (14:13-23)

- Imitate Christ (15:1-13)

*P*aul is very concerned that believers live in a community of love and grace for one very simple reason: We are the body of Christ in the world. The way we live together has a direct bearing on how Christ is perceived by non-Christians. If we condemn and judge one another, then the world will see Christ as condemning and judgmental. On the other hand, if we love and serve one another, the world will see Christ as a loving servant.

As you study this section of Romans, keep in mind that Paul isn't talking about major issues of your faith, such as those our church fathers fought for. We always need to guard against heresies (a heresy is an erroneous view—see 2 Peter 2:1) and false teaching. But when dealing with nonessential issues, such as those Paul discusses here, the operative word is *grace*.

Accept One Another (14:1-12)

Paul was definitely a multitasker. In addition to being a great missionary, a tentmaker, and a staunch defender of the truth, Paul was a part-time referee—he was forever trying to convince Christians that they should get along with and accept one another. In the church at Corinth, where Paul lived while he wrote his letter to the Roman church, people criticized each other over trivial matters (1 Corinthians 8). And although he had never been to Rome, Paul knew the believers there experienced similar problems.

The Weak and the Strong (14:1-4)

The problem with the Roman Christians was that two groups—the weak and the strong—were arguing with and judging each other, and this was causing division in the church.

Who Are the "Weak in Faith"?

Douglas Moo points out that the person who is weak in faith is not necessarily an immature believer. In the context of this passage, a weaker Christian is one who is hanging on to legalistic traditions. In the case of the Roman church, some people didn't believe that the Christian faith allowed believers to eat meat, drink wine, and ignore Jewish holidays.

What were the Christians in Rome arguing about? The first verse in Romans 14 defines it. Basically they were arguing over "disputable matters" (NIV). Another way to say it would be "doubtful things." In other words, they were arguing with each other over nonessential stuff. Two groups of people were involved in this debate:

- *Group #1*—These were the people Paul calls "weak in faith." They didn't think believers should eat meat (14:2) or drink wine (14:21), and they thought certain days of the week were more holy than others (14:5). These Christians tended to *judge* those they disagreed with.

- *Group #2*—These were those who were strong in their faith. They thought eating meat and drinking wine were okay, and they didn't think any one day was more holy than the others. These Christians tended to *despise* their weaker brothers and sisters.

Paul gets in the middle of both groups (like a referee) and says, "Look people, you need to get along." For Paul, the issue isn't eating or not eating meat. The issue is harmony. He wants both the weak and the strong to respect the views of the other and stop the fighting that is tearing apart the Christian community. Essentially Paul tells those who eat meat that they should not despise as narrow-minded those who don't eat meat. And those who don't eat meat are not to judge as worldly the ones who do.

Please the Lord (14:5-9)

Paul gives another example of a nonessential issue that was tearing apart the Christian community. This one has to do with what day of the week the Christians were setting aside to worship the Lord. Clearly, Paul doesn't take sides on the issue. However, this doesn't mean that Christians aren't supposed to have opinions. We should have convictions on these matters (14:5). We just shouldn't let them divide us. The overriding principle is that whatever we believe in these nonessential matters, we should live in a way that pleases the Lord and makes us want to give Him thanks (14:6).

Guidelines for Convictions

R.C. Sproul gives some excellent advice on how to have convictions, get along with other believers, and please the Lord—all at the same time!

1. You should arrive at your convictions after careful thought, study, and prayer. We need to know what we believe and why we believe it.

2. Regarding these "doubtful things" or nonessential matters of dispute, we need to understand that we can serve and honor the Lord with differing viewpoints.

3. When in doubt about doubtful things, we need to ask, "Does this please the Lord?" We also need to ask, "Can I enjoy this and thank God for it?"

The chief end of man is to glorify God and enjoy Him forever.

—*The Westminster Shorter Catechism*

The Judgment Seat of God (14:10-12)

If Paul's advice that we are to get along with one another isn't enough to convince us, he offers a more compelling factor: "Each of us will stand personally before the judgment seat of God" (14:10). This isn't the Great White Throne judgment all unbelievers will face (Revelation 20:11-15). All those who have been chosen, called, and justified through faith in Christ are no longer under condemnation (8:1). But we will face the "judgment seat."

The Greek word for *judgment seat* is *bema*. In the ancient world an athlete who won a race would walk up to the *bema,* which was a judge's bench, to receive an award. In the same way, all Christians will be judged by Jesus Christ on how many "races" they have won, spiritually speaking. Christ will judge our actions and the motives behind them. As Paul says, "Each of us will have to give a personal account to God" (14:12). Unquestionably, condemning, criticizing, or judging other Christians won't win us any heavenly rewards.

Don't Be a Stumbling Block (14:13-23)

Paul has just warned us not to condemn other Christians. But our judgmental attitudes aren't the only things creating division in the church. Our actions can also cause problems.

No Obstacles (14:13)

Often in Scripture you will see a verse like 14:13, where there is a command to stop doing something negative—in this case, "don't condemn each other anymore"—followed by a command to do something positive—in this case, "live in such a way that you will not put an obstacle in another Christian's path." Here Paul is addressing those who are "strong" in their faith (these are the meat eaters, the wine drinkers, the "I can worship God on any day" kind of Christians).

Both groups—the strong and the weak—can potentially put up stumbling blocks into the paths of others, but the strong are more likely to trip up the weak by what they do.

It's Not About the Food (14:14-18)

Paul comes back to the food to illustrate his point about obstacles. Paul is sure "on the authority of the Lord" that no food in and of itself is wrong to eat (Mark 7:18-19). But if you eat or drink something that offends another Christian or causes him or her "distress" (literally, it hurts or grieves them), then you are no longer acting in liberty and love but in selfishness and sin. As a Christian, you have a *right* to live freely before the Lord, but you also have a *responsibility* to your fellow believers.

The Christian and Freedom

Freedom brings with it responsibility. As a Christian you may be free to do certain things, but that doesn't mean you can violate other scriptural guidelines in the process. You can eat what you want, but you shouldn't eat to excess, because that would harm you and go against what Paul wrote about honoring God with your body (1 Corinthians 6:19-20). You may be able to drink what you want, but the Bible clearly commands us not to get drunk (Ephesians 5:18). And even if you are within those guidelines, you should always appeal to the standard of always acting in love.

Build Each Other Up (14:19-23)

In the end, the Christian life is not about what we can or can't do but about living in the control of the Holy Spirit, pleasing God, and building up others in the faith, maintaining harmony in the church. What Paul is saying here is that refraining from throwing obstacles in the path of our spiritual brother or sister is not enough. We need to live in such a way that we are encouraging others in their faith.

As for doing or not doing stuff, Paul has a final word or advice: When in doubt, leave it out.

Imitate Christ (15:1-13)

Remember when WWJD? was popular a few years ago? Unfortunately, a lot of people thought it was some big marketing campaign. Truth is, we have no better guide for our lives than to do what Jesus would do in any situation. In this section, Paul sets three different goals that will lead us to live in harmony with each other. In each case, he shows us Christ's example, which we are to imitate.

Live to Please Others (15.1-4)

By doing what pleases and helps others, we will build them up in the Lord. None of us should think so highly of ourselves that we aren't "considerate of the doubts and fears of others" (15:1).

> ***Christ's example:*** Read Philippians 2:5-8 to get a picture of what Jesus did for us. He didn't live to please Himself; He lives to serve others.

Live in Harmony (15:5-6)

The psalmist David wrote, "How wonderful it is, how pleasant, when brothers live together in harmony!" (Psalm 133:1). When Christians fight over nonessential issues, they send a terrible witness to the world. But when they live together in harmony, God is praised and glorified (15:6).

> ***Christ's example:*** Jesus always was in agreement with His Father. He always submitted Himself to His Father's will. And the Holy Spirit always glorifies Jesus. In the Godhead, we have the perfect example of harmony.

Accept Each Other (15:7-13)

R.C. Sproul writes that "accept" means "welcome." We need to literally welcome other Christians into our churches, our homes, and our lives. The body of Christ cannot be selective about friendships or care.

> *Christ's example:* Let's never forget that when we were sinners, Christ died for us (5:8). He welcomed us into His family even though we were His enemies. We need to follow the supreme and sacrificial example of Christ and accept each other.

◾ ◾ ◾

$\mathcal{S}$tudy the $\mathcal{W}$ord

1. Have you ever been judged by another Christian? Describe what happened. How did you feel?

2. Make a list of what you consider to be some essential Christian doctrines or beliefs. Make a similar list of what you consider to be some nonessential beliefs. Are any beliefs "on the fence"?

3. Now do the same thing for behavior. What, in your opinion, constitutes essential behavior? What behaviors are nonessential?

4. What issues divide Christians today? Which, if any, are essential beliefs or behaviors?

5. Why did Paul consider as weak those who believed that certain foods are unacceptable? (For more on the subject, read Jesus' view on this subject in Mark 7:18-19.) Is Paul trying to convince the weak believers to eat anything they want, or does he have something else in mind?

6. Read these passages on the judgment seat of Christ: 1 Corinthians 3:10-15; 2 Corinthians 5:10. How should this information impact the way you live?

7. Give a hypothetical example of one Christian throwing an obstacle into the path of another. Why is this so harmful?

8. How does following the example of Christ change your attitude and behavior? If you're not imitating Christ, who are you imitating?

Paul's "How to" Manual

The media are flooded with practical information about how to do almost anything. Do you want to know how to lose weight? You can choose from hundreds of books. Do you want to know how to transform your living room from a dump into a decorator's dream? Watch the Home & Garden channel. Do you want to know how to find an old high school classmate? Check out the Internet. How about this one: Do you want to know how to become an intentional Christian? Then study this last section of Romans.

Even though Paul may not have intended to give his readers a list of "here's how I did it" pointers (he was much too humble for that), he does tell us why he was so successful in his missionary efforts. Paul had a clear mission philosophy, he loved people, and he never lost his focus. Of course, his ultimate goal was to give God "the glory forever through Jesus Christ" (16:27), but he wasn't passive in the way he accomplished it. Paul was very intentional in all he did.

Do you want to become a more effective witness in the world? Study and adopt Paul's how-to manual presented here at the end of Romans.

Chapter 13

How to Be an Intentional Christian

Romans 15:14–16:27

What's Ahead

☐ Develop a Mission Philosophy (15:14-33)

☐ Love People (16:1-16)

☐ Stay Focused (16:17-27)

*P*aul must have known that his way of doing things—his "mission philosophy"—was effective, because he pretty much lays it out for his readers to see. This makes sense because one of Paul's purposes in writing to Romans was to teach and prepare believers to carry on his work.

As you go through this last chapter, think about what you are doing to carry on Paul's work. What is your own mission philosophy? What goals have you put into place? If you've never thought about being intentional in your efforts for Christ, Paul's how-to strategy is going to be a big help for you.

Develop a Mission Philosophy (15:14-33)

Here's the first how-to step in Paul's overall goal of being an intentional Christian. You need to develop a mission philosophy for your Christian life. In other words, what are the principles and beliefs that guide your life in Christ? Doing this will help you stay focused on your mission.

Paul's Mission Statement (15:14-19)

Paul had a clear-cut mission statement that can serve as a model for us. Notice the four main elements:

Identity (15:15-16)

Paul knew who he was in Christ: *For I am, by God's grace, a special messenger from Christ Jesus...*This should be a part of every Christian's mission statement. Even our name tells people who we are. We are *Christians!* We don't represent ourselves in the culture. We represent Christ. Paul wrote, "We are Christ's ambassadors" (2 Corinthians 5:20). An ambassador is a special representative, but the actual root of the word is from the Latin *ambactus,* meaning "servant." We are both representatives and servants of Christ here on earth. And we are here only by the grace of God.

Purpose (15:16-17)

Paul first stated his purpose to the Romans in 1:5, and he repeats it here: *For I am, by God's grace, a special messenger from Christ Jesus to you Gentiles...*Paul's purpose was to tell the Gentiles about the Good News of Jesus and to show them God's plan to bring Jews and Gentiles together in one body (Ephesians 3:6). This purpose energized Paul and created within him an enthusiasm for his work.

What is your purpose in serving Christ? Has God called you to witness to a particular group of people? Do you feel compelled to work through your profession? You need to figure that out and let it inform all you do. Without a clear purpose, you won't be motivated or enthused in your service to God.

Method (15:18)

After knowing your identity in Christ and your purpose in serving Him, you need to have a method. In other words, how are you going to carry out your purpose? Paul's method was two-pronged: *For I am, by God's grace, a special messenger from Christ Jesus to you Gentiles by my message and the way I lived...*Paul's message was the Good News, of course, and he delivered it by preaching and writing, both of which he could do very well. But as good as he was, Paul also needed to live an exemplary life. How often have we seen in our own day a wonderful message get buried because the messenger's life was a poor example?

What about your message? Do you have a firm grip on what you believe and why you believe it? And how are you delivering your message? Do you talk to people one-on-one, or are you comfortable speaking to groups? Are you a writer, an artist, a filmmaker, or a Web designer? We all have communication gifts, but are we using them to communicate the message of Christ to the world around us? And how about the lives we lead? Are they giving our message credibility or getting in the way?

Power (15:19)

Paul's power to do what he did came from the Holy Spirit, and so should ours: *For I am, by God's grace, a special messenger from Christ Jesus to the Gentiles by my message and the way I lived. I have won them over by the miracles done through me as signs from God—all by the power of the Holy Spirit.* When you see the word *miracles* here, don't just think of things like healing, although God is still in the healing business. Think instead of the miracles God has already done in your life through the Holy Spirit, and how these were signs to others that God is real. If you are depending on the Holy Spirit and letting Him control your life, then you will see miracles, and others will notice. If you aren't living daily in the Holy Spirit's power, then you won't experience what Paul is talking about.

Paul's Mission Statement

For I am, by God's grace, a special messenger from Christ Jesus to the Gentiles by my message and the way I lived. I have won them over by the miracles done through me as signs from God—all by the power of the Holy Spirit.

Paul's Mission Strategy (15:20-22)

Once he had developed a mission statement, Paul plotted out a strategy. He was very intentional about the things he did and the places he visited. By this time in his life Paul had been spreading his message to the Gentiles for ten years, always with this strategy in mind: "to preach the Good News where the name of Christ has never been heard" (15:20). Paul's strategy was to be a pioneer for Christ.

The value of a strategy is that it guides your ambitions and actions, and prevents you from duplicating the efforts of others. If you want your gifts and the way you use them to be even more effective, develop a carefully devised plan of action.

Paul's Mission Itinerary (15:23-33)

At first glance this section appears to be a simple schedule of Paul's travel plans. But if we look below the surface, we see that it is much more than that. Paul was being very intentional about the *places* he was going to visit and the *purpose* for going to each one.

From Corinth to Jerusalem (15:25-27)

Paul really wanted to go to Rome (15:23-24), but first he wanted to deliver a gift from the church in Corinth to the church in Jerusalem. The Corinthian Christians, who were mainly Gentile, felt indebted to the Jerusalem Christians, who were mainly Jews. They knew that their spiritual blessings had come to them through the Jews, so they wanted to pay on this debt by contributing to the more impoverished church in Jerusalem.

To Italy and Spain (15:24)

This shows the far-reaching nature of Paul's strategy. The Bible doesn't tell us if Paul ever reached Spain, but don't bet against him. Tradition says that after Paul was released from two years of house arrest in Rome (Acts 28:30), he set out on a fourth missionary journey before being recaptured, imprisoned in Rome again, and finally executed by Nero. We do have a hint from Clement—a Roman Christian and a companion of Paul (Philippians 4:3)—that Paul made it to Spain. In his own letter to the church at Corinth, Clement writes this about Paul: "To the whole world he taught righteousness, and reaching the limits of the West he bore witness before rulers."

*Ɛ*xtraordinary *T*ravel

John Stott calculates that all of these journeys Paul writes about at the end of Romans would have added up to at least 3000 miles. "When one reflects on the uncertainties and hazards of ancient travel," writes Stott, "the almost nonchalant way in which Paul announces his intention to undertake these three voyages is quite extraordinary." It's no wonder that he urged the Roman Christians to pray for him (15:30-32).

Love People (16:1-16)

You might be tempted to skip over the last chapter of Romans because it seems to read more like a phone book than a field manual. True, most of the chapter contains greetings from Paul to people he knows personally or by reputation, but it also contains insights into the mind, the heart, and the methods of this great man of God. It also shows that Paul was intentional about loving people.

Paul's Scrollodex

Paul must have had some kind of system to keep track of people. Although he had never been to Rome, he knew a whole bunch of people there. The reason for this, no doubt, is that Paul had met many of these people in such major cities as Antioch, Corinth, and Athens. That they ended up in Rome is not surprising. Rome was the capital of the empire, and all roads really did lead there. What you have to be impressed with is how carefully Paul kept track of his friends. In today's terms, he would be considered a great networker. Far from being some philosophical hermit or lofty theologian, Paul was a true friend to many people.

Paul's Heart

The language Paul uses in his greetings gives us a glimpse into his heart. He loved these people! And he encourages the church to do the same. He tells them to greet each other in "Christian love" (16:16). The NIV says, "Greet one another with a holy kiss," a common custom in the Ancient Near East. However we greet and treat each other, we should do it with the love of Christ. That's what Paul has in mind for us because it's what Jesus wants for us. Jesus said, "Your love for one another will prove to the world that you are my disciples" (John 13:35).

Stay Focused (16:17-27)

This is the third leg of Paul's success formula for intentional Christian living. In any kind of endeavor, focus is critical. Losing concentration or letting down your guard can be costly, especially if you're involved in life-and-death situations. Okay, so maybe we aren't on the front lines of a war zone, where a lack of focus can literally cost you your life. But we are on the front lines of a spiritual war zone. As Paul wrote to the Ephesians:

> *For we are not fighting against people made of flesh and blood, but against the evil rulers and authorities of the unseen world, against those mighty powers of darkness who rule this world, and against wicked spirits in the heavenly realms* (Ephesians 6:12).

If we are in Christ, we know what's going to happen in the end: "The God of peace will soon crush Satan under your feet" (16:20). In the meantime, we have to "watch out for people who cause divisions" (16:17), and we must "stay innocent of any wrong" (16:19). An intentional Christian is alert and vigilant. The believer who wants to please God can't be sleeping on the job.

If we had to do this on our own, none of us would stand a chance. But God is able to make us strong (16:25). As Paul wrote to the Philippians, "I can do everything with the help of Christ who gives me the strength I need" (Philippians 4:13).

And why do we do all of this? In order to give God the glory He deserves (16:27). The famous hymn by Fanny Crosby probably says it best:

> To God be the glory, great things He has done!
> So loved He the world that He gave us His Son,
> Who yielded His life an atonement for sin
> And opened the Lifegate that all may go in.

■ ■ ■

$\mathcal{S}$tudy the $\mathcal{W}$ord

1. As best you can, write out your own personal mission statement. Don't try to make it perfect. You will probably be working on it for a while.

2. Do you have a purpose in serving Christ? What drives you spiritually?

3. What kind of message are you delivering to others? Think about this in terms of your life as well as your words.

4. Why should a Christian do everything with excellence? What happens when Christians produce second-rate products? What happens when Christians run second-rate companies? What can you do to get better in your chosen field or profession?

What can you do to get better at explaining your Christian faith to others? See 1 Peter 3:15-16.

5. What kinds of miracles has God done in your life and through your life?

6. Have you developed a strategy for your life? In one paragraph, summarize your goals for the next ten years. Include your spiritual and ministry goals as well as your professional goals, and show how you will integrate them.

7. What practical lessons from this passage can you learn about loving and building up people?

Dig Deeper

*W*henever we write a book about God and His Word, we do a lot of research and reading. These are the main books we used to write this Bible study on Romans. If you want to dig deeper into Romans and the Bible, here's a great place to start.

Commentaries

The Message of Romans by John R.W. Stott is a wonderful and very thorough commentary. Stott has the ability to bring out scholarly truths without getting bogged down.

One of our favorite New Testament Bible scholars is William Barclay. He's down-to-earth yet deep (a rare combination). We used his book, *Romans,* from The Daily Study Bible Series.

The Life Application Bible Commentary series is outstanding, and *Romans* was a big help. This commentary has plenty of what the title says—application.

R.C. Sproul explains Romans in his excellent *Tabletalk* study, which relied on the classic commentary on Romans by James Montgomery Boice.

If you like books that are organized around detailed outlines, then you will like *Exploring Romans* by John Phillips.

The MacArthur New Testament Commentary Series volume on Romans is word-for-word and very in depth. John MacArthur is especially good at word studies.

If you want to know about the history and the culture of Bible times, you will love the *Zondervan Illustrated Bible Backgrounds Commentary.* The New Testament comes in four volumes. We used volume 3, which includes the excellent commentary on Romans by Douglas Moo.

The New Testament volume of *The Bible Knowledge Commentary,* edited by John Walvoord and Roy Zuck, also provides valuable background and historical information.

Likewise, the New Testament volume of *The Bible Background Commentary* by Lawrence Richards is a great Bible study tool.

One of the best Bible commentary sets is the *Expositor's Bible Commentary.* It's a bit more scholarly than the others, but sometimes you need a little more in-depth analysis. We used volume 10, which includes Romans by Everett F. Harrison.

General Bible Study Helps

We wrote two books on the Bible we found helpful in writing this Bible study. Check out *Knowing the Bible 101* and *Bruce & Stan's Guide to God.* They are written in the same "user-friendly" style as this book.

Adventuring Through the Bible by Ray Stedman is another excellent resource.

Bible Translations

Obviously you can't study Romans or the Bible without the primary source—the Bible! People often ask us, "Which Bible translation should I use?" We recommend that your primary study Bible be a *literal* translation (as opposed to a paraphrase), such as the *New International Version* (NIV) of the Bible or the *New American Standard Bible* (NASB). However, using a Bible paraphrase such as *The Living Bible* or *The Message* in your devotional reading is perfectly acceptable.

Our personal choice is the *New Living Translation* (NLT), a Bible translation that uses a method called "dynamic equivalence." This means that the scholars who translated the Bible from the original languages (Hebrew and Greek) used a "thought for thought" translation philosophy rather than a "word for word" approach. It's just as accurate but easier to read. In the final analysis, the Bible that's best for you is the Bible you enjoy reading because you can understand it.

We used the NLT for just about all of our references in this Bible study. However, you will notice that we occasionally used the NIV and the NASB. And a couple of times we even went back to the classic King James Version of the Bible (KJV).

A Word About Personal Pronouns

When we write about God, we prefer to capitalize all personal pronouns that refer to God, Jesus, and the Holy Spirit. These would include *He, Him, His,* and *Himself.* However, not all writers follow this practice, and nothing is wrong with that. In fact, personal pronouns for God were not capitalized in the original languages, which is why you'll find that most translations use *he, him, his,* and *himself.*

Bruce and Stan would enjoy hearing from you. Contact them with your questions, comments, or to schedule them to speak at an event.

Twelve Two Media
P.O. Box 25997
Fresno, CA 93729-5997

E-mail: info@christianity101.com

Web site:
www.twelvetwomedia.com

Exclusive Online Feature

Here's a Bible study feature you're really going to like!
Simply go online at:

www.christianity101online.com

There you'll find a Web site designed exclusively for users of the Christianity 101 Bible Studies series. When you log on to the site, just click on the book you are studying, and you will discover additional information, resources, and helps, including...

- *Background Material*—We can't put everything in this Bible study, so this online section includes more material, such as historical, geographical, theological, and biographical information.

- *More Questions*—Do you need more questions for your Bible study? Here are additional questions for each chapter. Bible study leaders will find this especially helpful.

- *Answers to Your Questions*—Do you have a question about something in your Bible study? Post your question and an "online scholar" will respond.

- *FAQ's*—In this section are answers to some of the more frequently asked questions about the book you are studying.

What are you waiting for? Go online and become a part of the Christianity 101 community!

Christianity 101® Bible Studies

Genesis: Discovering God's Answers to Life's Ultimate Questions

"In the beginning" says it all. Genesis sets the stage for the drama of human history. This guide gives you a good start and makes sure you don't get lost along the way.

1 & 2 Corinthians: Finding Your Unique Place in God's Plan

This enlightening study explores the apostle Paul's helpful responses to issues that churches continue to face today: maintaining unity in the church, exercising spiritual gifts, and identifying authentic Christian ministry.

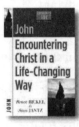

John: Encountering Christ in a Life-Changing Way

This study reveals who Jesus is by demonstrating the dramatic changes He made in the lives of the people He met, including Nicodemus, the woman at the well, Lazarus, and John, "the disciple whom Jesus loved."

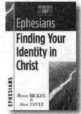

Ephesians: Finding Your Identity in Christ

Verse for verse, the book of Ephesians is one of the most profound, powerful, and practical books in the Bible. This guide reveals the heart of Paul's teaching on the believer's identity in Christ.

Acts: Living in the Power of the Holy Spirit

Bruce and Stan offer a fresh look at the ongoing ministry of Jesus through the church. They highlight the drama of the early Christians' triumph over darkness and their explosive growth from a band of 120 fearful followers to a thriving, worldwide church.

Philippians/Colossians: Experiencing the Joy of Knowing Christ

This new 13-week study of two of Paul's most intimate letters will inspire you to know Christ more intimately and maintain your passion and vision. Filled with helpful background information, up-to-date applications, and penetrating, open-ended questions.

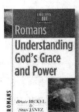

Romans: Understanding God's Grace and Power

Paul's letter to the church in Rome is his clearest explanation and application of the good news. This fresh new study of Romans assures you that the Gospel is God's answer to every human need.

Revelation: Unlocking the Mysteries of the End Times

Have you ever read the final chapters of the Scriptures, only to finish with more questions than answers? Bruce and Stan help you understand Revelation's encouraging message and apply it to your life today.

Christianity 101® Series

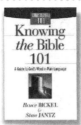

Knowing the Bible 101
Enrich your interaction with Scripture with this user-friendly guide, which shows you the Bible's story line and how each book fits into the whole. Learn about the Bible's themes, terms, and culture, and find out how you can apply the truths of every book of the Bible to your own life.

Creation & Evolution 101
With their distinctively winsome style, Bruce Bickel and Stan Jantz explore the essentials of creation and evolution and offer fascinating evidence of God's hand at work. Perfect for individual or group use.

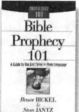

Bible Prophecy 101
In their contemporary, down-to-earth way, Bruce and Stan present the Bible's answers to your end-times questions. You will appreciate their helpful explanations of the rapture, the tribulation, the millennium, Christ's second coming, and other important topics.

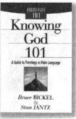

Knowing God 101
This book is brimming with joy! Whatever your background, you will love the inspiring descriptions of God's nature, personality, and activities. You will also find straightforward responses to the essential questions about God.

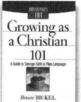

Growing as a Christian 101
In this fresh new look at the essentials of the Christian walk, Bruce Bickel and Stan Jantz offer readers the encouragement they need to continue making steady progress in their spiritual lives.

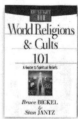

Word Religions and Cults 101
This study features key teachings of each religion, quick-glance belief charts, biographies of leaders, and study questions. You will discover the characteristics of cults and how each religion compares to Christianity.

Bible Answers to Life's Big Questions
Bruce and Stan invited readers to e-mail their questions about Christianity, and after receiving more than ten thousand, they still answer every one. Now you can read these representative e-mails and the clear, concise answers about God, the Bible, the Christian life, and more.

Bruce & Stan's® Pocket Guide Series:

AVAILABLE FROM TWELVE TWO MEDIA:

To order these Pocket Guides,
visit www.twelvetwomedia.com

Bruce & Stan's® Pocket Guide to Prayer

This very portable guide to prayer is as fun to read as it is uplifting. Readers will experience the wonders of communicating directly with God as Bruce and Stan explore the truth about how and why to pray.

Bruce & Stan's® Pocket Guide to Islam

Cutting through the mystery of Islam, Bruce and Stan's look at the world's second largest religion will help Christians better understand and witness to Muslims. Includes information about the Koran and Muslims' beliefs about Christ.

Bruce & Stan's® Pocket Guide to Knowing God's Will

Here, the wise and witty Bruce and Stan help readers discover the practical realities of hearing God, discerning His will, and walking in His perfect plan. Easy-to-understand explanations, highlighted with eye-catching graphics.

Bruce & Stan's® Pocket Guide to Knowing the Holy Spirit

The Holy Spirit often seems a most mysterious person. Bruce and Stan explore the many dimensions of His role in our lives. Covers "quenching the Spirit" and how to avoid it, and helpful ways to hear the Holy Spirit's voice.

Bruce & Stan's® Pocket Guide to Knowing Jesus

Using charts, sidebars, and information icons, this concise guide answers questions about Jesus and clarifies misconceptions about salvation, faith, and grace. Addresses the "all God, all-man" mystery, and the amazing truth of Christ's resurrection.

Bruce & Stan's® Pocket Guide to Studying Your Bible

Bruce and Stan cut through difficult concepts, unfamiliar customs, and awkward names to make Bible study accessible and fun. Readers will explore Bible organizations, translation differences, and effective ways to apply God's truths.